In Praise of
The Strangeness of Truth

"Fr. Ference's *The Strangeness of Truth* is a gift. With pathos and humor, he explores the wisdom and beauty of Catholicism—its faith in the non-competitive God, its embodied character, its transformation of suffering and death through Christ's cross and resurrection—in light of his own experience as brother, son, student, rock fan, and priest. I warmly recommend it, especially for young people searching for life's deepest truths."

—Bishop Robert Barron, founder of Word on Fire
Catholic Ministries, Auxiliary Bishop of the
Archdiocese of Los Angeles

"Fr. Damian Ference is one of my favorite people. Like, ever. He's humble, articulate, and winsome. All of that comes through in this excellent little book that gives the reader an overview of the Catholic faith in a fresh and compelling way. I wish I had it back in my agnostic days."

—Matt Fradd, *Pints With Aquinas*

"Read this book and fall in love, or grow more in love, with Jesus and His Church!"

—Fr. Larry Richards, pastor of St. Joseph Church and founder of The Reason for Our Hope Foundation, Erie, Pennsylvania

"*The Strangeness of Truth* is a stirring call to make our faith not just a place we visit, but rather the very air we breathe, the food we eat, and the home in which we live. I have long been convinced that Fr. Damian Ference will be remembered as one of the greatest spiritual thinkers of this generation, and this work more than bears that out."

—Hallie Lord, SiriusXM radio host and author of *On the Other Side of Fear: How I Found Peace*

"Fr. Damian has long been one of my favorite writers, and this book only affirms that. Weaving together saints, stories, philosophy, and faith, he paints a picture of Catholicism that is both fresh and accessible. Anyone reading this book will see how Catholicism makes sense of life and makes it tangibly better. Give this book to anyone who doubts that."

—Brandon Vogt, founder of ClaritasU and author of *Why I Am Catholic*

The Strangeness of Truth

The Strangeness of Truth

Vibrant Faith in a Dark World

Fr. Damian Ference

BOOKS & MEDIA

Boston

Library of Congress Cataloging-in-Publication Data

Names: Ference, Damian, author.
Title: The strangeness of truth : vibrant faith in a dark world / Damian Ference.
Description: Boston, MA : Pauline Books & Media, 2019.
Identifiers: LCCN 2018038239| ISBN 9780819891266 (pbk.) | ISBN 0819891266 (pbk.)
Subjects: LCSH: Catholic Church--Doctrines. | Theology, Doctrinal--Popular works.
Classification: LCC BX1754 .F47 2019 | DDC 230/.2--dc23
LC record available at https://lccn.loc.gov/2018038239

Published by Pauline Books & Media, 50 Saint Pauls Avenue, Boston, MA 02130-3491.
www.pauline.org

Printed in the U.S.A.

Pauline Books & Media is the publishing house of the Daughters of St. Paul, an international congregation of women religious serving the Church with the communications media.

1 2 3 4 5 6 7 8 9   23 22 21 20 19

For Helen,
the one and the many.

"It is the business of the artist to uncover the strangeness of truth."

—Flannery O'Connor

Contents

Foreword

IT IS WITH GREAT JOY that I write this foreword to this absolutely wonderful book, *The Strangeness of Truth: Vibrant Faith in a Dark World*, by Father Damian Ference, a dynamic priest of the Diocese of Cleveland, who is also a seminary professor, a philosopher, a loving son, brother, friend, and a spiritual guide for many. More than simply a book, it is a moving letter to those who search and yearn for meaning. It speaks to those who are restless, who are filled with questions and looking for answers to the many challenges and contradictions that we all find in the course of our journey. *The Strangeness of Truth* is a profound reflection on the treasures of the Catholic faith, seen and presented through the eyes and heart of the personal journey of the author. As a young man, Damian Ference encountered the Risen Christ in a powerful way. This encounter would eventually lead him to leave behind his youthful dream to be a "rock star" and to give his life to Jesus Christ and all of humanity as a priest in the Catholic Church. He is now a star of a different kind, much like the Star of Bethlehem. Today, Father Damian shows the way to others, the way to a life of faith in the person and vision of Jesus Christ who, after all, is the Way!

In this book, written as a moving letter to all of us who search, we can see the unfolding of our own lives. We follow Father Damian through life, with all its ups and downs, twists and turns, as he shares the stories of his own life and faith journey. Through it all, he discovers meaning and purpose in the treasure of the Catholic faith. In so many ways, this is a book about two of Pope Francis' favorite words: *encounter* and *accompaniment*. In *The Joy of the Gospel*, Pope Francis invites all of us to a renewed personal encounter with Christ, or at least an openness to letting him encounter us. He reminds us that no one is excluded from this invitation and that the Lord does not disappoint.

The Strangeness of Truth. How can Truth be strange? Father Damian tells us how. Sandwiched in the narratives of his story, this book shares with us the surprising story of the intimate encounter of God with us, his people. It is the story of how he demonstrates the power of his love. God's love is a love that accompanies us in creation, in the mystery of dying and rising, and even through the signs and symbols of our faith, which are always reminding us that "everyone counts and everyone matters." Father Damian presents the beauty of the Catholic faith to us artfully and skillfully, in a language and through images that are understandable and relatable. He shows how faith enlightens and gives meaning to our lives and the many events that arise in them. Through it all, we are given the opportunity to discover the footprints of Christ, who is and has always been there, right by our side.

My prayer is that all who take the time to read this book from a young, faith-filled priest, will discover what he has discovered and be transformed by the love of Christ, who seeks to encounter us at every turn. Thank you, Father Damian, for taking the time to share your story, for presenting us the treasures of the Catholic faith, and for giving us this book as a gift to the world!

Most Reverend Nelson J. Perez, D. D.
Bishop of Cleveland

Why This Book?

"Go and announce the Gospel of the Lord."

— *Roman Missal*

"I invite everyone to be bold and creative in this task of rethinking the goals, structures, style, and methods of evangelization in their respective communities."

— *Pope Francis*

"When you can assume that your audience holds the same beliefs as you do, you can relax a little and use more normal means of talking to it; when you have to assume that it does not, then you have to make your vision apparent by shock, to the hard of hearing you shout, and for the almost blind you draw large startling figures."

— *Flannery O'Connor*

DEAR READER, THIS LITTLE book is my humble attempt to present the Catholic faith to you for the first time, or for the first time in a long time, or perhaps in a way that you haven't heard it presented before. I am writing to you not only as a Catholic priest but also as a man who has come to find himself most fully alive in communion with the One who is Life itself, and in the Church that he founded almost two thousand years ago.

I was ordained one year after the clergy sex-abuse scandals rocked the Catholic Church in 2002, so I am not blind to the human weakness, hypocrisy, cowardice, greed, and arrogance that is at times on display in Catholic living. But I've also been an eyewitness to the kindness, courage, honesty, generosity, and humility of countless women and men who profess Jesus Christ as Lord and refer to the Catholic Church as their *Mother* and *Teacher*. I believe what the Catholic Church holds and teaches to be true, and this book is my attempt to present the beauty, the mystery, the challenge, the consolation, and the joy of Catholicism to you in an honest, human, intelligent, humorous, and incarnational manner.

Perhaps you were raised Catholic but haven't been practicing your faith for a while. This book is for you. Perhaps you went to Catholic grade school and high school or even Catholic college but stopped practicing your faith a while back because it didn't seem relevant to your life anymore. This book is for you. Perhaps you once had very strong faith and then life came at you with terrible suffering through the death of a loved one, sickness, a break in a most important relationship, or some existential crisis. This book is for you. Perhaps you are new parents who have decided that your son or daughter needs to be raised in a faith that has greater wisdom and values than the world has to offer. This book is for you. Perhaps you are a student and your teacher or professor wants you to read something that presents Catholicism in way that ties personal narrative and theology together. This book is for you. Maybe you are a seeker, a searcher, a man or woman who is on a journey looking for answers to questions about the meaning of life in general and Catholicism in particular. This book is for you. Perhaps someone who loves you very much gave this book to you as a gift and you are wondering if it's for you. It is.

The structure of this book is simple; it's like a sandwich. I begin each chapter with a narrative from my own life. That's the bottom bun. Then I offer a systematic treatment of a particular topic: the incarnation, the resurrection, sacramentality, the human person, exemplarity, beauty and reason, the both/and principle, and suffering. That's the protein, cheese, lettuce, tomato, onion, and condiments. Finally, I close each chapter with another narrative, which relates to the narrative with which I began the chapter. That's the top bun. If you don't like carbs, skip the narratives, and if you're a carb loader, you can simply read the buns. But the best diet is a balanced diet, and the buns are whole grain, so the best way to read this book is by reading the entire chapter. You could skip around if you want, but each chapter really does build on the next, so read this book the traditional way, from beginning to end, and then pass it on to a friend so that you'll have someone with whom you can discuss the book over a cup of coffee or a pint of beer. (By its nature, Catholicism is communal, so it's good to discuss these matters with others. You might even want to read this book aloud to another and work on the discussion questions in Appendix 2 together!)

Happy reading!

Fr. Damian Ference

God Is for Us, God Is with Us

Incarnation

"And the Word became flesh."

— *John 1:14*

"God became not only a man, but Man."

— *Flannery O'Connor*

IN THE EARLY EIGHTIES, a Saturday morning at the Ference house translated into a morning of chores. After breakfast, my mom and dad would present to my brother and me a list of things to be done around the house. Then we'd all get to work.

Being the youngest, I always thought the way my parents distributed chores between my brother and me was anything but fair. Because Adam was four years older, he got to do all the fun stuff, like cutting the grass and washing the cars. I was stuck weeding the gardens and trimming the grass around the flowerbeds with hand clippers, not with the gas-powered trimmer that I use today. I also had the terrible charge of picking up after our beloved dog, Peanuts.

Peanuts was a Labrador-mutt mix that we adopted from the Animal Protective League when I was four. My mom used to tell me that we saved his life—I guess the pound would have killed him if no one took him. Naturally, I was attached to my dog. When I was really young, I used to sit on his back and make him carry me around our living room like a horse. (Years later, my cousins would blame me for his arthritis.) I liked everything about Peanuts—well, almost everything. The only thing that I didn't like about my dog was cleaning up after him on Saturday mornings. He'd drop bombs all over the backyard during the week, and it was my job to find each one and pick it up in order to clear the way for Adam and his lawn mower.

What made this chore even worse was that Adam would take great delight in watching me work. Having already cut the front lawn, he'd watch me survey the backyard with shovel in hand, searching for poop. My dad had told me that using the corner of the shovel made the job easier, and he was right. Yet as I cleared the yard, Adam would offer color commentary and gloat, reminding me to "get everything!" The smell and sight were bad enough, but having your older brother ride you about it was the worst.

But he'd get his. What Adam didn't realize was that while he was busy giving me the business about finding every last piece of poop in the yard, I would strategically leave one fresh pile for him, his mower, and his shoes. So when he ripped the cord and restarted the lawn mower, it was my turn to gloat.

A few minutes into cutting the back grass, he'd stop, mid-yard. With the mower still running, he'd bend his leg back and turn his head over his shoulder to check the bottom of his shoe. His face would sour. Ha! He felt it. He smelled it. It ruined his morning. And it made mine.

My brother and I were always going at it. Everything was a competition, and both of us hated losing. Nobody likes losing. Nobody.

We human beings tend to think that God is somehow competing with us. It may be hard to admit, but it's true. If we're honest with ourselves, we have to confess that something deep down inside of us makes us believe that, somehow, God is waiting to pounce on us, kind of like the way my brother and I used to pounce on each other as kids. Sometimes we may think that God doesn't want our best, that he's simply waiting for us to mess up, make a mistake, or break some commandments in order to throw lightning bolts our way.

Have you ever had the feeling that God is out to get you? Although the notion of God as a competitor is a popular one, and we may even feel it at times, it's not true. It's actually the furthest thing from the truth.

Here's the truth: God has no need to compete with us because God is God. What the heck does that mean? It means that God is not a part of the world. And by "the world" I don't just mean the earth, I mean the entire universe and every created thing. I mean the context of everything that is. Before anything ever existed, God existed. God has no beginning or end. God just *is*. God is not a thing—God is God. Thomas Aquinas called God *the sheer act of existence*. God is existence itself.

God is also love. Aquinas defines love as *willing the good of the other, for the sake of the other*. Love is not directed toward the self but to the other, as other. Love involves making a sincere gift of oneself for the sake of another person. Love wants what's best for someone else. The Greek word *kenosis* means self-donation or self-emptying. Love is donating or emptying one's self for the sake of another person. Love is *kenosis*. Love is always directed toward the other. But how can God be love if there is only one God? Doesn't God need somebody to love? Doesn't God need an other? And if God needs something, wouldn't that make God less than God?

It is true that love is only possible with more than one person. After all, love has to be given and received. As they say, *it takes two*. That's what makes love love.

Take a husband and wife, for example. A husband loves his wife—he is her *lover*, she is his *beloved*. As the lover, he gives himself completely to her—he empties himself. As the beloved, she freely receives him and she loves him back, emptying herself to him completely. He, in turn, receives her love, the gift that is her very self. Such is a mutual exchange of love. Both the husband and the wife freely give themselves to each other and freely receive each other as gift. But there's more. In addition to the husband and the wife, there is also the *love itself* that is being exchanged between them, which can manifest itself in another person! So the reality is that love doesn't take two, it actually takes three—*the lover*, *the beloved*, and *the love in between*. Love is a communion of persons. Love draws us into relationship with others.

Does any of this sound familiar? It should. If God is existence itself, there can be only one God, because existence by its nature is one. In other words, there cannot be two Gods who are each infinite existence, because one would limit the other, and then neither would be infinite. And if God is love, and if love is only possible between persons, then there must be three persons in this one God. Human reason by itself could not have come up with this idea. It came to us from God by means of divine revelation. This is what we mean by the mystery of the *Trinity*. The Father loves the Son, as the Father is the *lover*. (He did not create the Son. The Son was always there; he is eternal like the Father. That's what we mean when we say "begotten not made" in the Creed.) The Son receives the Father's love, as the Son is the *beloved*. The Son also gives his love to the Father, and the Father receives the Son's love. And who is proceeding from the Father and the Son? What do we call the love in between the lover and the beloved? You've got it: the Holy Spirit. The Father, Son, and the Holy Spirit are one in being, or one in substance. Or, to use the language in our Nicene Creed, they are *consubstantial* (literally, "with one substance"). Therefore, God is one, not in the unity of a single person but in a Trinity of persons, each of whom fully possesses the one divine substance or nature. God's nature is love. And God is love because God is a communion of persons: Father, Son, and Spirit.

Moreover, if God is one as a Trinity of one substance, and if God is a communion of persons, a communion of love, that means God is *self-sufficient*. In other words, God doesn't need anybody to love because God is love itself. Because the Father loves the Son, and the Son loves the Father, and the Holy Spirit is the love proceeding from the Father and the Son, God has no needs. Why is this important? Because it means that God created the world not out of need but out of love. God didn't have to create the world—he wanted to create it, and he created it out of love. And if that's true, then why would God want to compete with his own creation? That wouldn't make any sense. He'd always win.

Okay, that was a lot all at once and you may need to read this section over a few times more before it sinks in. Don't feel bad if that happens. Remember that the Trinity is a profound and eternal mystery. It's not a post on social media. You can't explain it in 280 characters. It's not like a math problem either. Math problems can be solved. You can't solve the Trinity. If you could, it wouldn't be a mystery. You contemplate mystery. You sit with it. You rest in it. Understanding takes time—so take your time. But also know that this stuff is really important. If we don't get the Trinity right, then we're going to get everything else wrong, including ourselves.[1]

In addition to God being a Trinity of persons, God is also Creator. God created all things visible and invisible, and he created all things *ex nihilo*, out of nothing. This is a wild reality because it means that before there was time, space, atoms, molecules, motion, and light, there was God. Lots of people get this wrong. They tend to think that God is part of the world rather than the Creator of the world. This distinction has enormous consequences.

When God created the world—and again, when I say "world" I mean everything that exists—he created it not because he had to but because he wanted to. God created the world out of love. God chose to create—he willed the world to be. And although everything that God created reflects his goodness, the pinnacle of his creation was man and woman—of course, that means you and me.

God created us in his image and likeness. And that means that we are like God in a way that no other creatures are like God. We have a body (visible) and soul (invisible). We also have intellect and free will. We can know and we can choose. We can know the difference between right and wrong, good and bad, true and false. And we have the freedom to act on that knowledge. We can also know God, and we can choose to love or turn away from God. Animals are different from us in this way.

Animals don't have reason or free will, which means that animals can't do things like murder or rape. Humans can. When an animal kills, it kills for food and survival. When a human being kills, it may be for a variety of reasons. We make distinctions about how and why humans kill in a way that is unique to human beings. We make a distinction between self-defense, manslaughter, and murder. We make a distinction between marital love, hooking up, and rape. Animals don't. They can't.

Animals are also unable to love. You love your dog, but your dog can't love you back. I know that sounds harsh. Although dogs seem to show some sort of affection, and people can be very attached to their dogs, it's different from true love, which is only between persons. Let's go back to our definition of love: *willing the good of the other, for the sake of the other*. Only a human being can will anything, because only human beings have free will. Therefore, only human beings can love. Love is *kenosis*; it's self-donation, self-gift. Love is a personal act. It takes persons to love.

If you go back and reread the second and third chapters of Genesis with all this in mind, it will make a lot of sense. Recall that God created the man and the woman not because he needed to but because he wanted to. He created Adam and Eve out of love and for love. He wanted to enter into a loving relationship with them—to become one with them, just as a man and woman become one with each other. God didn't force them into relationship—they entered into relationship freely; they chose it.

Remember the tree of knowledge of good and evil that God planted in the garden? Lots of folks wonder why God planted that thing. Was God tempting the man and the woman? If so, that's cruel. Some folks think that if that tree weren't there, then original sin would not have occurred, meaning that the Fall was all God's fault. Others think that the tree was the source of freedom, and that eating from it made the man and woman human. Neither of these are good interpretations.

The point of the tree in the story is actually to represent human freedom. It shows that loving God is a choice, an act of the will. Love is a decision. That tree symbolizes the opposite of loving God. To eat of that tree is to reject God. To eat of that tree is to die. Although choosing to eat from that tree will never make us free, the tree itself is necessary for real freedom. The tree represents our ability to choose something else besides God. Loving God is a choice, and so is turning from him.

Sin emerges from the belief that God is against us, that God is our competitor. That's the lie the serpent tells to the woman (and the man) in the third chapter of Genesis. He convinces them that God is their competitor and that if they really want to be free, if they really want to live, they need to reject God and embrace something else. To reject God and embrace something else is a human act—it's a choice. It's what we call *sin*. And indeed, that's what they choose. Rather than trusting God and choosing to love him, they turn from him, because they think that by turning from him they'll be free. It doesn't happen. It can't happen. Yet because we keep thinking that it will happen, God decides to show us that he's on our side.

To save us from this thing we call sin, God sent us his only Son. Why? Because we can't save ourselves from sin. Christianity is not a self-help religion. We can't simply pick ourselves up by the bootstraps and give it the old college try. Perhaps you've learned this the hard way. Have you ever done everything in your own power to try and fix yourself or heal yourself but still came up short? I have. It didn't work. Sin runs deep, so deep that we need a Savior to rescue us from it.

It's really important to note how God saves us from sin. He doesn't save us abstractly. He doesn't save us by sending an angel down to earth or some sort of super human. Nope. He sends us his only Son, the Second Person of the Trinity, who becomes one of us in all things but sin. Again, this is something that we are familiar with as a statement of fact, but not something we often think about or contemplate in the fullness of its reality.

Christians believe that God, who is totally other, all good, all knowing, all powerful, self-sufficient, and eternal, actually humbled himself and became a human being. That's ridiculous. Really, it is. We often become so comfortable with nativity scenes and Christmas songs that tell the story of the incarnation, how God became a human being, that we completely miss the reality of what is one of the most important moments in human history.

When I was a kid, I attended Incarnate Word Academy from kindergarten through eighth grade. Although my teachers, the Sisters of the Incarnate Word, explained a few times what our school's name meant, I never gave it much thought.[2] My friends and I just called it "IWA" and that was that. That's sad. My school was named after the reality that God became a human being, which is a profound mystery, but to me, it was simply the name of my Catholic grade school.

When it comes to the incarnation, it's imperative to remember that God is not our competitor. God is self-sufficient in the communion of persons that is the Trinity. God doesn't need to save us—God wants to save us. And to show us that he's come to save us, he comes in a way that is credible and convincing—he comes as one of us because of love.

Jesus Christ is fully God because he is the Second Person of the Trinity begotten of God the Father. He is also fully human because he is born of the Virgin Mary, a human being. (More on Mary in Chapter 4.) Jesus Christ is one person—a divine person, the Son of God— with both a divine nature and a human nature. Think about that for a moment. If it doesn't blow your mind, then you haven't thought about it hard enough. Jesus Christ is both God and man, both at the same time.

How is the incarnation possible? How can God become one of us without demolishing our humanity? After all, God is completely other, and we define God by what we are not. God is perfect, good, all-knowing, all-powerful, and immortal. God always was, always is, and always will be. We, on the other hand, are not perfect, not all-good, not all-knowing, and we are mortal. How can God and man come together like that? How can two contrary things come together as one? It is only possible because of who God is. And remember, God is not our competitor. God is self-sufficient. God doesn't need anything. When God becomes a human being in the person of Jesus Christ, his divinity does not overtake his humanity. Jesus Christ is both fully God and fully man at the same time. Since God is not our competitor, his divinity does not challenge our humanity. And since God created man for communion and not for competition, in the person of Jesus Christ we see how God is and wants to be with us. He doesn't come to compete, he comes to save—he comes to be with us, even in our brokenness and sin. God is Emmanuel. God is with us.

The two most popular and recognizable depictions of Jesus Christ the Incarnate Word are him *in the cradle* and *on the cross.* Both images are a beautiful testimony to the reality that God is for us and with us. God is not against us—He is not out to get us. God comes to save us.

Saint Luke tells us that Jesus was born in a stable in Bethlehem, which should strike us as funny. If God were to come among us, wouldn't it be more appropriate for him to be born in some pristine castle, surrounded by guards, a protective moat, and solid walls? Or wouldn't it make more sense for him to be born in a more sterile location than a barn or cave? Of all places, a stable sounds like the last place in the world that the Son of God should be born. So, why a stable?

Stables don't always smell good, and they can be chaotic and messy. The same can be said of our hearts and our lives.

Life is difficult and at times heart-wrenching. We live in a fallen world. Yet that is where Jesus comes to meet us, right in the middle of that mess we call sin. God is born right in the middle of the messiness of our lives to show us that he is with us, that he is for us, and that he can save us from ourselves. Jesus Christ is born in a stable to show us that he's not afraid to enter the messiness of our broken lives. He gets us. He's one of us. And because he is also God, he can save us.

Something similar happens on the cross. The last place you would expect to see God incarnate would be on an instrument of torture and death, but sure enough, that's where we find him. Jesus Christ, the Son of God, the innocent one, dies a terrible death by crucifixion. Why? Isn't it below God to do such a thing? Yes. That's the point. God humbled himself so much in the person of Jesus Christ that he was willing to die a terrible death so that we might live. *Kenosis.*

The cross is dark, messy, and painful, yet we find Jesus Christ, the Son of God, right in the middle of it. That's intentional. Because God is for us and with us, Jesus shows us the lengths that he will go to prove that he is not our competitor but our Savior and Friend. The cross symbolizes our fallen world, and Jesus is not afraid to enter directly into the eye of the storm and conquer death itself by entering into death on the cross.

The other important feature of the cradle and the cross is that both images are non-threatening and non-competitive. A baby is powerless. A baby needs to be fed, held, burped, and changed. A baby can't hurt you. A baby can't compete with you. The same is true of a dying man on a cross. He can't do anything for himself—he can't even get himself a drink. The crucified Christ is powerless, just like the newborn Christ. Both are signs and reminders of the non-competitive nature of God.

Jesus comes to us not to hurt us or to take away our freedom or to scold us, but to heal us, to love us, and to save us. The Incarnate Word empties himself completely in the cradle and on the cross so that we might trust him and allow him to save us.

I began this chapter about the Incarnation with a story about me, my older brother, and dog poop. I told it to highlight our competitive nature as fallen human beings and to show that we often bring that idea of competition to our understanding of God, which is actually a misunderstanding of who God is and what he is about. God is not our competitor—God is our Creator and Savior. God is for us and with us. I want to end this chapter with another story about poop in order to serve the same purpose.

The people of Catalonia, Spain, like most Christian peoples, decorate their homes and churches during the Christmas season with Nativity scenes. Like all Nativity scenes, the figurines of Jesus, Mary, and Joseph are at the center of the action in the middle of the stable. The other players vary, but usually shepherds, Magi, and a variety of animals fill out the rest of the scene. But the Catalonian people add another character to the mix: *El Caganer* or "The Crapper."

I first heard about the tradition of *El Caganer* a couple of years ago and couldn't believe my ears. But it's true. Most Catalonian Nativity scenes host a figurine of an elf-like man with a funny red hat who is off in the distance, somewhere out in the fields (never in the stable itself) with dropped drawers, taking a poop. It's silly, shocking, and embarrassing. But it's also humbling, human, and incarnational. When God entered into our fallen world as one like us in all things but sin, he entered into every part of being human.

For the Catalonian people, *El Caganer* is a theological reminder of the shocking nature of the incarnation—that when God took on our nature in the person of Jesus Christ, he entered into everything human. Everything. *El Caganer* also reminds us that God enters into our world as things are, as we are, wherever we are. Jesus comes to meet us in order to save us, not to embarrass or compete with us. He is for us and with us.

El Caganer is a strange image indeed. But for a faith that proudly, regularly, and rightly depicts the God of the universe as a baby in a diaper and as a man dying on a cross, should this really be a surprise?

2

The Empty Tomb

Resurrection

"He is not here, for he has been raised just as he said."

— *Matthew 28:6*

"The resurrection of Christ seems the high point in the law of nature."

— *Flannery O'Connor*

MY MOM NEVER KNEW me as a priest. She died a little over a year before I was ordained. She battled cancer on and off for the last fifteen years of her life.

She won her first fight back in 1986, but not without losing a breast and a good amount of hair. As the consummate underdog, she won her second fight ten years later, but she lost her ovaries and uterus in the brawl. Two years after that she fought and won her third battle, and for a while I thought my mom was the champ. After three intense rounds, she was tired, but the cancer was not. It went to her liver. She was sick of fighting, and the only reason she went one last round was because my dad and my brother and I asked her to. The chemo didn't work. Her doctor said she had from two to six weeks to live. After spending fifty-three weeks at a cancer home, she died, surrounded by the Dominican sisters who took care of her, along with me, my dad, my brother, and my pastor. It was a Saturday morning. I cried.

When we got home, we didn't know what to do. Mom was dead. I washed my car while listening to Jeff Buckley's *Grace*. My brother Adam smoked cigarettes and talked about funeral plans. And my poor, legally blind dad just walked aimlessly around the house, picking up things that reminded him of my mom. At one point he approached my brother and me with my mom's prosthetic breast and asked, "Sons, what should I do with this? Should I give it to Saint Vincent de Paul?" Adam said, "Nah, Dad. You hold on to that one." It was a strange morning indeed.

Death is like a knuckleball—even when you know it's coming you're never really prepared for it. If you've lost someone you love, you know what I mean. I knew my mom was dying, but I didn't know what it was like for her to be dead until she actually died. And then all those things you've imagined—like the wake and funeral and burial—really happen.

Much of the wake is a blur. But I do remember being happy to see folks I hadn't seen in a long time and to meet folks I had never met before, folks who knew my mom and told me great stories about her that I had never heard. I also distinctly remember people I didn't know ignoring my brother while making a big deal of me because I was a seminarian. That didn't sit well with me, so at one point I said to my older brother, "Play along." For a few minutes I pretended to be Adam and introduced strangers to my brother, the seminarian. People fawned over him and told him how proud my mom would have been. Being the sibling of a priest or seminarian isn't easy, and I wanted my brother to know I knew that. Yes, it was silly, but we were grieving. I've confessed it since.

The funeral Mass was beautiful. Over thirty priests concelebrated, and the church was pretty full with a wide variety of folks who wanted to pray with us, for us, and for my mom. In his homily, my pastor mentioned that my mom's name meant "*gift from God.*" That sounded right. But, like the wake, it went by quickly and I don't remember many other details.

And then there was the burial. Of all the things that happened immediately after my mom died, I remember that least. The only thing I recall was that at the end of the prayers of committal my pastor added, "And now we pray a Hail Mary for the next one of us who will die." I liked that a lot, but it made some people uncomfortable, especially my seminary professors, which is probably why I liked it.

My mom's body is buried at Holy Cross Cemetery, just below the spot that had been bought for my dad, right next to the bodies of my Grandma and Grandpa Ference, immigrants from Slovakia. My dad didn't marry my mom until he was forty-six, and so my grandparents bought him a burial plot when they bought their own. When my dad married my mom, a woman fourteen years younger than he was, everyone figured that she would outlive him. So when my mom died first, we had to buy the land below my dad's plot. And that's where her body rests. And as of May 31, 2016, my dad's body rests over hers.

Most people are familiar with the basic story of Christianity. We covered it in Chapter 1. God the Father sent his only Son to the world out of love to save it from sin. In order to do that, Jesus had to die. He had to enter death to save the world from death. And his death was quite brutal. He died at the hands of political and religious leaders by way of crucifixion, which was a terrible form of public humiliation, torture, and execution.

The death of Jesus was a scary thing. Jesus was the preacher, the teacher, the prophet, the healer, the friend, the peacemaker, and the lover. He was also the Savior—he was the Son of God and he was God. Jesus was innocent, yet he unjustly suffered a criminal's punishment. And his death was unspeakably violent, so much so that most of his friends couldn't bear to watch.

It's easy to forget all this. After all, the cross and the crucifix are the most common symbols of Christianity. Every Catholic church is supposed to have a crucifix in its sanctuary, and most Christian churches have some form of the cross in their worship space. People wear crosses as jewelry, tattoos, and on T-shirts, often without giving much thought to the meaning of the ancient symbol.

I was about eight or nine years old when I first started to consider the strangeness of the cross. My intrigue was likely inspired by one of the sisters from Incarnate Word Academy in a third grade religion class, but I don't really remember. I do remember telling my mom that if Jesus was stoned to death instead of being crucified, we would make the *sign of the stones* rather than the *sign of the cross*, and then I started poking my torso over and over with my stiffened hands. My mom laughed and affirmed my insight. So I decided that I should share my theological reflection with my dad. He got really upset and told me that I shouldn't talk that way about our Lord. I liked my mom's response better. She knew that I was on to something.

The point is that Jesus was killed, and that is a historical fact. He was dead. The soldiers charged with the actual crucifixion knew as much. Rather than breaking his knees to speed up his suffocation like they had done to the two criminals on either side of Jesus, they pierced his side with a lance just to make sure. The spear pierced his heart, and blood and water flowed out. Yep. He's a goner. Finished. Bye-bye, Jesus. You've been killed. Death won. You lost. Game over. Maybe.

Death sucks. You can't do much about it. You can deny it, but then you're living in fantasyland. Eventually, you just have to accept it as a brute fact of life. Everybody dies. Everybody.

And death hurts. No one wants to die. Even people who kill themselves really don't want to die as much as they want to stop hurting. Death is loss, and loss is separation and division. Death divides a unity that once existed. A person you once knew and loved and talked to and hugged is no longer a person but a corpse. Sure, we embalm bodies and fix up their hair and cake on the makeup, but no matter what anyone says, no one looks good in a casket.

Sometimes during wakes at the funeral home people will say, "Oh, he looks so good, so peaceful." I want to say, "Really? Because he looks pretty cold and dead to me." And why shouldn't he? He's dead. I never say these things aloud, but sometimes I want to.

I remember my six-year-old nephew telling me, "That doesn't look like Grandpa" when he first saw my dad at his calling hours. Mike was right. The undertaker had filled in my dad's cheeks and put a lot of makeup on him. As a priest, I've grown comfortable with wakes, but the truth is that I'd much rather keep company with someone in her last days in hospice than with a dead body in a funeral home. Death is spooky. It turns people into corpses. Jesus' corpse was pinned tightly to the cross until a courageous man named Joseph of Arimathea asked if he could have it. The authorities obliged. So Joseph took Jesus' shredded, bloody body down from the cross and wrapped it in a linen burial cloth. It must have been pretty gross. As a priest, I've seen a lot of death and it's never pleasant. God bless Joseph. He also placed Jesus' corpse in a rock-hewn tomb in which no one had yet been buried. Then he rolled a stone against the entrance of the tomb to seal it, just like we would cover a casket with six feet of dirt. Jesus' mom and a few other women were there too. It must have been devastating for them as they watched Joseph bury the body of the one they loved. It must have hurt. And from what Scripture says, it seems like the women just sat there and watched, not knowing what to do. Could you blame them?

I felt the same way after my mom died. Not knowing what to do, I washed my car, my brother smoked, and my dad wanted to know what to do with a prosthetic breast. If you've lost someone you've loved, you've felt it too. An emptiness and a sadness just lingers there. It's heavy and it hurts. In a way, it paralyzes you for a while. You need to grieve, you need to heal, and you need to keep going. But your beloved is gone and you can't change that. Death sucks.

Imagine for a moment that a few days after we buried my mom I went back to Holy Cross Cemetery to visit her grave and grieve. I knew they hadn't put the headstone in place yet, and having gone to plenty of funerals and burials, I also knew that her plot would be easy to find, as it would stand out from the others as a rectangle of freshly packed dirt amidst grass and headstones. But now imagine that as I was walking to her grave, I noticed a few big piles of dirt on either side of the rectangular hole that was my mom's burial plot. Imagine that as I ran over to the hole and looked down into it, I saw an open casket but no body. What would you do? What would I do? I'd probably cry, or throw up, or for the first time in my life I might even faint. After coming to, I'd ask, "What the heck happened to my mom's body? Who dug her up? What kind of sick person would steal a corpse?"

Of course, this scenario didn't happen to me. My mom's body is still buried safely within the earth of Holy Cross Cemetery. But this scenario did happen—it happened to the close friends of Jesus. Recall that Joseph of Arimathea had put Jesus' body into the tomb on Friday and a stone was rolled before it and sealed. Saturday was the Sabbath, and visiting the dead was forbidden on the Sabbath. So early Sunday morning, a few of Jesus' good friends went to visit his tomb.

Mary Magdalene, Joanna, and Mary, the mother of James, came to the tomb Sunday morning at dawn. You wonder if they even slept the night before. It must have been hard to celebrate the Sabbath after having watched one of your best friends get demolished on a cross a day earlier. You may know how it is after you see something horrible. You play it over and over again in your head and try to make sense of it. Did the women walk in sorrowful silence to the tomb? Did they talk to each other? If they did, what sorts of things did they say? Did they recall their favorite memory of Jesus? Did Mary Magdalene tell the other two about the time Jesus drove out her seven demons and made her a new woman? Did the women share their memories of the last conversation they had with him before he died? Did they recall his last words from the cross, just like we recall the last words of our loved ones just before they die? Did they talk about how terrible his body looked hanging mangled on that cross? Did they talk about how reverent and dignified Joseph was in taking his body down from the cross and wrapping it with care and confidence? Did they talk about his mom and the terrible grief that she was going through? Did they cry? Did their cries ever turn into laughs, the way they do among mourners? Who knows? But whatever conversation they were having, if indeed they were having one at all, would have stopped upon their arrival at the tomb. What they saw was shocking.

They found the stone rolled back from the tomb. They looked inside. Jesus' body was gone. Thieves! Robbers! Body snatchers! Sick people! Who would steal a corpse and why? Damn Romans.

But it gets weirder. The next thing they know, two men in bleached garments are standing beside them. Are these guys the thieves? Nope. But they do have a question for the women: "Why do you search for the Living One among the dead? He is not here—he has been raised up." Then the two men proceed to quote Jesus, reminding the women that he used to talk about having to suffer, die, and rise again. Not knowing exactly what was happening, but knowing that something had happened, the women went back to tell the others.

Until this point in history, no one had ever beaten death. So even imagining what "rising again" might look like was difficult, if not impossible. Jesus had brought two people back to life during his public ministry: Lazarus and Jairus' daughter. But those weren't *resurrections*—those were *resuscitations*. The difference is that when somebody is dead and you bring her back to life, she still has to die eventually. Most of us have heard of people who have died and were brought back to life. Nikki Sixx, the bass player from Motley Crue, loves to tell the story about how he died from a drug overdose and, thanks to a great medical staff, got another chance at life. This sort of thing is called resuscitation—people come back to life in the same body with which they died, and they go on living the way they lived before. But they will eventually have to die again. Even after Jesus resuscitated Lazarus and Jairus' daughter, both of them eventually died again.

But resurrection is different. It had never happened before, and although Jesus predicted his own resurrection, and although some of the Jews believed in the resurrection of the body, no one had ever seen it. But those two men in the tomb told the women that Jesus had been raised. What did that mean?

Often when we think of someone coming back from the dead, we think of something like a ghost or a zombie. A ghost is simply a spirit (without a body) and a zombie is simply a body (without a spirit). Both are pretty scary. Although zombies are fictional, a ghost could be an apparition of a soul in purgatory. It is a murky area, however, and the Church is opposed to any dabbling in the occult. There is something incomplete and unresolved about both ghosts and zombies because human beings are both body and spirit, not one or the other. No one wants to be a zombie or a ghost. No one wishes that their dead friends will one day return as zombies or ghosts. But we all want to see our loved ones again, just like Mary Magdalene and her friends wanted to see Jesus again, just like I want to see my mom again, just like you want to see your beloved dead again. The best-case scenario would be to see them resurrected. And the best-case scenario is what happened to Jesus.

The first time Mary Magdalene caught sight of the risen Jesus, she didn't recognize him. She thought he was the gardener. And why would she recognize him? The last time she saw him he was a bloody pulp. This guy looks different. So she asks the supposed gardener to tell her where Jesus' body is, thinking that he might have taken it. She goes on to say that she'll carry his body back to the tomb. It's a funny scene because a corpse is heavy and who knows how she would have done it. But she didn't have to, because the next thing you know, Jesus calls her name: "Mary." Boom! With that, she knew it was him. She knew his voice. She knew how he said her name. She responded by calling him "Teacher" and then embraced him, not wanting to let go. Could you blame her?

When you imagine what the perfect reunion with a deceased loved one would look like, how do you imagine it? When I think of seeing my mom again, I don't think of her as a ghost or a zombie. I don't think of her weighing seventy-eight pounds, her face all gaunt and her body like a skeleton, which is what she looked like in her final days. No, I think the best possible scenario would be to see her with her body but better, healthy, and new. As a matter of fact, since my mom was sick for a good part of my life, the photo I keep of her in my bedroom is one when she was in her mid-thirties, maybe a year before I was born. She's sitting on a picnic bench, smiling and healthy. That's so much better than a ghost or zombie.

When more people started to encounter the risen Jesus, they had a similar reaction to that of Mary Magdalene. At first, they didn't recognize him. And again, why would they? If you witnessed someone die and watched his burial, you wouldn't expect to see him walking the earth again. But that's exactly what happened. And that's the craziest and best thing that the world has ever witnessed. It changed the world. It changed human history. Jesus Christ was crucified, died, and was buried, but he returned from the dead not as a zombie or ghost but as his glorified self. He is risen. He has a body—a glorified body. He will never die again. He beat death. And that's a big deal.

Catholics celebrate funerals well—even non-Catholics, non-Christians, and atheists say so. Our ritual and liturgical tradition is comforting and consoling. Why? Because we have a reason to hope. Because we believe in the resurrection. Because Christ is risen. Because Jesus promised that those who die with him will also rise with him. Because we have the courage to believe all of this. Because it's true.

Catholics understand that death is a part of life. We know that death sucks—it's hard. And it can be very, very sad. But we also believe that death, which is the great equalizer, has been beaten. Death has lost its sting. The fact that Jesus Christ rose from the dead changed everything. It changed the history of the world. It changed people. It made a coward like Peter willing to preach with a confidence that allowed him to lay down his own life for the belief in Christ's resurrection. It allowed Paul to do the same, not to mention Agnes, Lucy, Anastasia, Perpetua and Felicity, John and Paul, Cosmas and Damian. All those folks were willing to die because they knew that death had been conquered once and for all, and that they too had the promise of living forever with Jesus in a new way, with glorified bodies, not bound by time and space.

If Mary Magdalene and those early disciples had found Jesus' body in the tomb that Sunday morning, no one would care about him today. We wouldn't be talking about him. Jesus would be just another historical figure who was a "good guy" and had some nice teachings, but there would be no reason to build a whole religion around him, not to mention to date the years by him. No, if he never rose from the dead, then his life really wouldn't matter and half of the things he said would have been lies. But if he did rise—and our faith teaches that he did— then it does matter. And it matters for everybody. It even matters for you. Shouldn't it?

3

Matter Matters

Sacramentality

"He spat on the ground and made clay with the saliva, and smeared the clay on his eyes."

— *John 9:6*

"What is visible in our Savior has passed over into his mysteries."

— *Saint Leo the Great*

WHEN I WAS A NEWLY ordained priest, I met Jen and Frank, a young married couple with five children. They were parishoners at Saint Mary's Parish, my first assignment. Their two youngest children, Caroline and Sophia, were twins. Since they weren't yet old enough for preschool, Jen would bring the twins along with her when she ran errands around town. Often, those errands included a stop at Saint Mary's.

I remember the twins being shy, especially around me. They both had big blue eyes, but they often would hide behind their mother's legs to avoid eye contact or any potential conversation. One day, as Jen was making her way back to my office with Caroline and Sophia, one of the ladies in the office offered the twins some candy, which they gladly accepted. A few minutes later, sitting in my office, Caroline looked at her mom with eyes wide open, dropped her jaw, and threw up all over Jen and my office chair. (It turned out that Caroline was allergic to peanut butter.) Caroline started crying, so Sophia started crying, while Jen calmly apologized for the crying and the puke. Then she proceeded to wipe Caroline's face clean with a baby wipe. I called maintenance.

One reason that Jen was in my office that day was because she and Frank had been struggling with the Church's teaching on birth control and she was seeking some counsel. Having five children it wouldn't seem like they used birth control, but they did, although not always carefully. Jen had confessed contraception and had received some wildly diverse advice from priests. One said, "You have five children. You have been open to life. Don't ever confess this sin again." She left the confessional in tears, knowing in her heart that what the priest said to her wasn't true. (Why did her conscience bother her so much if contraception wasn't a sin?) Another priest told her that contraception was the worst of sins and that she and Frank needed to stop immediately or face the pains of hell. Again, she left in tears. This priest acknowledged the sin, but offered her no hope, consolation, comfort, understanding, or pastoral advice.

The other reason that Jen was in my office was because she worked in youth ministry. She was chosen to present the Church's teaching on sexuality, including contraception, homosexuality, and all the other hot-button issues. She told me that she didn't think she could teach this to the teens because she wasn't convinced of the Church's teaching on some of those issues. Fair enough. We found someone else to teach the teens those topics. But we still hadn't solved Jen's dilemma.

I had studied Paul VI's controversial encyclical *Humanae Vitae* in college seminary and again in graduate seminary, and I knew what the Church taught about marriage and marital love. It was 2003 and, although a little late to the game, I had just started studying John Paul II's *Theology of the Body*. I knew the Church's teaching theoretically, but I was now in a pastoral situation with a beautiful Catholic mother in front of me looking for answers. So we started studying, talking, and researching, looking for satisfying answers to some very serious questions about love and life. Of course, Jen and Frank were on their own journey as a married couple, but as their priest, I was along for the ride.

Abstract doctrines are one thing, but lived experience is another. Reading *Humanae Vitae* and *Theology of the Body* is one thing, but putting Church teaching into action is easier said than done. Doing well in seminary ethics and moral theology courses is a good thing, but it's not the same as putting those theories into action with a flesh-and-blood couple sitting before you. Words are one thing, but for words to really matter they need to take on flesh.

If there's one thing that we've learned so far, it's that in Catholic Christianity, matter matters. Stuff matters. Bodies matter. When God came to us in the person of Jesus Christ, he didn't come to us as an angel or an abstract idea. God came to us as one like us in all things but sin. God took on our flesh. God became incarnate. (It all started when he was conceived in Mary's womb, and then it continued at his birth in the stable of Bethlehem.) God chose to communicate himself to us *through* and *in* and *as* a human being. In other words, God uses matter, or stuff, to communicate himself to us.

Think about Jesus' earthly ministry. He was constantly entering into people's lives with his life—he wasn't afraid to get messy or use things from nature to carry out his ministry. Remember the story of the man born blind? How did Jesus heal him? He spit on the ground, made some mud, and wiped it on the man's eyes! Or how about the deaf man? Jesus stuck his fingers in his ears, spit, touched the man's tongue, looked up to heaven, groaned, and said, "*Ephphatha!*" which means, "Be opened." And the man's ears were opened. Even the leper was cured because Jesus stretched out his hand and touched him saying, "Be made clean." Jesus isn't afraid to enter in, to get messy, to use his own body to encounter us.

Over and over again in the Gospels Jesus enters places that are fallen, and he raises them up. For the couple that ran out of wine at their wedding reception in Cana, he turns water into wine, and it's the best wine ever. And he makes more than they could possibly need. The woman at the well, who still hadn't found what she'd been looking for, finally finds it in the person of Jesus, because he's willing to meet her where she is and love her in a way that she's never been loved before. The fishermen who can't catch a thing haul in the biggest catch of their lives after Jesus instructs them to throw their nets over the other side of the boat. This is who Jesus is and what Jesus does, and, notice, he does all of it with and through his body. In other words, everything Jesus does is incarnational. He physically enters into people's space. He enters into their lives. There is nothing abstract about Jesus. He makes God's presence known through his person because he is a divine person with both human and divine natures.

God meets us where we are in the person of Jesus Christ in order to take us to where he is. Since it's hard to come to know the invisible, the invisible becomes visible so that we can better know him. This is the beauty of the incarnation and the incarnational nature of the Catholic Church. For example, it's one thing to say that our lives are meant to be given away as gifts, but it's another thing entirely for God to come to us in the flesh of Jesus and literally give his body to us as a gift on the cross, completely emptying himself—his life, his breath, his blood, his tears, his sweat—for the sake of his beloved. It's one thing to say that God wants to give his life to us, but it's another thing for God to actually make himself present in the form of bread and wine so that we can literally eat and drink him.

As Catholics, we believe that God communicated himself to us most perfectly and beautifully in the person of Jesus Christ, and he continues to communicate himself to us now incarnationally through stuff. We call this stuff the Sacraments. Jesus initiated all seven Sacraments during his ministry and, through the power of the Holy Spirit, the Church has been encountering God through them for the past two thousand years.

Like the person of Jesus Christ, the Sacraments of the Catholic Church are not abstract. They are all very earthy. It makes sense that if God communicated himself to us through the person of Jesus Christ, then his mode of continuing to communicate with his people would be incarnational as well. Just as people in the Gospels first came to know Jesus through their senses, the Sacraments first speak to us through our senses. Sacraments are sensual, in the literal sense of the word. Thomas Aquinas (following Aristotle) says that we first come to know things through our senses. In the Sacraments, we come to know God's love and grace through water, oil, bread, wine, and bodies. In other words, God pours himself out to us through the mediation of stuff. The world is fallen, but it's good, and so God uses the stuff of the world to recreate the world and to make us his own.

John the Baptist baptized Jesus in the waters of the River Jordan. When Jesus came up from that water, the heavens parted and the Spirit descended upon him like a dove and a voice from heaven said, "You are my beloved Son; with you I am well pleased" (see Lk 3:22). But if baptism washes away sin, and if Jesus is like us in all things *but* sin, why did he get baptized?

Baptism is the starting point of Jesus' public ministry. In a sense, his baptism prefigures his death and resurrection. He goes down into the river and comes back up—it's a preview of Good Friday and Easter Sunday. It's the formula of Christian living: dying and rising. It's the Paschal Mystery. Jesus is baptized not because he needs to have sin washed away; he is baptized to make the water holy so that we can have our sin washed away by entering into his Paschal Mystery, his dying and rising.

In the Bible, water is both a sign of death and a sign of life. Water is scary and it's refreshing. Water can drown. Water can kill. On the other hand, life is impossible without water. Everything alive needs water in order to live. Water also can make us clean. Whether our clothes, our car, or our bodies, water allows us to clean things, to make them new again and to refresh them.

It should be no surprise then that when the Catholic Church welcomes new people into the Church community we do so with water. Rather than simply shaking someone's hand and saying, "Welcome, you're in," we follow Jesus' instruction to his apostles and bring folks into the Church through water. And people get wet.

A Sacrament is a sign given to us by Jesus that allows us to experience his grace, which is God's love in action. And since we have bodies, the Church celebrates Sacraments in a way that informs the whole person, not just the mind, that something is actually happening. Sacraments are incarnational. Baptism is incarnational.

When someone gets baptized, not only does the priest or deacon say, "I baptize you in the name of the Father, and of the Son, and of the Holy Spirit," he also accompanies those words with bodily action! He dunks the person in water, or at least pours some water over her head. Why? Because being dunked in water or having water poured over you speaks to you (body and soul) in a way that words alone could never communicate. The water (especially if it's cold!) shocks the body and says, "Something new is happening here!" Sacraments are never simply a mental or purely spiritual activity—they are personal and incarnational.

What does Baptism do? By going down into the waters of Baptism we die with Jesus. Sounds morbid, I know. But new life, the life of grace, is not possible without death. You can't fill a cup with freshly brewed coffee unless you first pour out the nasty day-old coffee that's left in the cup. Likewise, unless we empty ourselves and die with Jesus, he can't fill us up with his love and live in us. And in Baptism, that's what happens. The baptismal water is a living symbol that calls us to die with Christ so that we can live with him in the community he established, which is what we call the Church.

Baptism also gives us an identity. Just as the Father said to Jesus, "You are my beloved Son—with you I am well pleased" as he came up out of the Jordan, the Father says the same thing to every person who is baptized. This is a very big deal. It means that we become God's sons and daughters through Baptism, and it also means that God is pleased with us. In other words, we find our true identity in the waters of Baptism.

Baptism reminds us that we are not our sins; we are the sum of the Father's love for us, as John Paul II used to say. God loves us and delights in the very fact that we exist. We are beloved sons and daughters of the Father. In fact, in Baptism we actually become "other Christs." This is why the newly baptized wear a white garment; it's a sign of new life in Christ. It's also why they receive a candle; it symbolizes Jesus, the light that entered into the world to save it from the darkness of sin. Notice how incarnational these symbols are. As Catholics, we don't just tell the newly baptized that they are a new creation and that they are called to be a light in the world, we actually give the newly baptized brand new clothes and a lighted candle after they come up from the baptismal waters. After all, water matters, clothing matters, and fire matters.

Oil matters too. In the sacrament of Confirmation, a baptized person is sealed with the gift of the Holy Spirit. This is normally done by a bishop. As with Baptism, Confirmation is incarnational; it speaks to the whole human person through word and symbol—in speech and in stuff.

First, the bishop lays his hands on the head of the person to be confirmed. This laying on of hands is an ancient symbol for the descent of the Holy Spirit upon the Apostles at Pentecost. Think about that for a moment. As Catholics, we don't just say, "May the Holy Spirit descend upon you," we actually embody it! Why? Because we come to know things through our senses, and the fullness of the sacramental life can never be experienced simply through words.

After the laying on of hands, the bishop then takes some perfumed oil known as "chrism" and he makes a cross on the person's forehead with it, saying, "Be sealed with the gift of the Holy Spirit." Not only can the one being confirmed *see* the bishop before him and *feel* his thumb making the sign of the cross on his head with the newly applied oil, he can also *smell* the oil and *hear* the bishop's voice. Sacraments by their nature are sensual, never simply spiritual.

Bread and wine matter too. Jesus came to save us from the darkness of sin, from our own selfishness. He accomplished this by giving his life away, by emptying himself on the cross. On the night before he died, he gathered his apostles and took bread, broke it, and said, "This is my body, which will be given up for you; do this in memory of me." And then he took the cup and said, "This cup is the new covenant in my blood, which will be shed for you" (see Lk 22:14–20). The very next day he literally gave up his body and poured out his blood on the cross of Calvary.

In the sacrament of the Eucharist, Christ makes himself present at every Mass in the bread and the wine, which cease to be, at their deepest level, bread and wine, and become the true presence of his Body and Blood. That sounds crazy, but it's true. The same God who sent us his only Son as a baby in Bethlehem and allowed him to die a brutal death on a cross also allows him to be present to us in the simple gifts of bread and wine in the Eucharist. Communion can never be an abstract concept for Catholics. We actually become one with God and one another by literally consuming the Body and Blood of Jesus in the Eucharist. We can *see* the host, *smell* it, *feel* it, and *taste* it. That's real communion in the most incarnate sense. There's nothing abstract or cerebral about it.

Bodies also matter. In the sacrament of Marriage, a man and a woman physically enact the dramatic union between Christ and the Church. It sounds funny, but one of the things that I have to ask a couple as part of their marriage preparation is whether or not they are impotent, that is, whether they are physically able to engage in sexual intercourse. Why in the world would I need to know that? Because when a man and a woman receive the sacrament of Marriage, it is not simply a social contract but an embodied covenant. In their wedding vows, a man and a woman promise each other at the altar that they will love each other unconditionally, no matter what—but it's not enough to simply say it. They have to show it. The marriage isn't quite official until it is consummated through marital intercourse—the husband and wife need to become one in more than simply words. And when they come together bodily in a way that mirrors Christ and his Church, God's grace abounds.

Speaking of marriage, one of the best ways to understand the sacrament of Holy Orders is by way of a marital analogy. Jesus often referred to himself as the Bridegroom—we, the Church, are his Bride. He comes to marry us, to be one with us, to give himself to us, to pour his life out for us, and, in a word, to love us. Jesus entrusted his Church to the Apostles and gave them power and authority to carry out his mission by serving the Church. When a man is ordained, he is marked in a unique way to stand in for Christ the Bridegroom "and possesses the authority to act in the power and the place of the person of Christ himself."[1] A bishop or priest brings Jesus to his people in preaching, teaching, and celebrating the Sacraments. And he does all of this *through his (male) body*, which might seem obvious, but it often goes underappreciated. Not only did God humble himself to come among us as a man; not only does he humble himself to be present in bread and wine in the Eucharist; not only does he humble himself to be present in the procreative union of husband and wife, but he also chooses to humble himself to be uniquely present in some very unworthy men through the sacrament of Holy Orders.

In addition to standing in for Jesus the Bridegroom in the celebration of the Eucharist, another important charge of the priest is to offer his Bride forgiveness and healing through the sacraments of Reconciliation and Anointing of the Sick.

Reconciliation, often simply known as Confession, is a stumbling block for lots of folks. They ask, "Why can't I just tell my sins directly to God and let that be that? Why do I have to go to a priest?" These are good questions. But another good question is, "Why would God give us the sacrament of Reconciliation and use a priest to offer us his healing love?"

If you know anyone in a twelve-step program, or if you're in one yourself, you know that the first step to recovery is admitting that you have a problem. And you actually have to stand up and admit that you have a problem out loud to other people. It's not enough to write it in your journal or whisper it to yourself as you're trying to fall asleep. Both of those actions are a good way to start, but until you take ownership of your weakness and admit that you can't fix or heal yourself, you remain hurt. The same holds true for the sacrament of Reconciliation. The priest stands in the person of Christ and in the person of his Church to offer healing in a very real and incarnational way. In other words, just like every other Sacrament, there is nothing abstract about Confession. Jesus gave the Apostles the power to forgive sin, and that power is present in every priest, and it's present for us. To actually confess your failings and weaknesses to another person can be humbling, but it's also liberating, especially when you know that God has chosen a fellow sinner as his unworthy instrument to extend his healing and forgiveness. There is something very comforting and real about hearing that "your sins are forgiven" spoken by the real, embodied voice of one who humbly stands in the person of Christ and his Church to assure you that it's true. God gives us the sacrament of Reconciliation not because *he* needs us to confess our sins to a priest but because *we* need to.

Anointing of the Sick is closely connected to Reconciliation, and it also exists for our sake so that we can tangibly experience Christ's healing power. Consider this: Your grandma just had a stroke and was rushed to the hospital. She's been Catholic her whole life and has been a great model of faithfulness for you and your family. You call the rectory and tell your pastor about what happened to your grandma. The pastor says, "Okay, I will pray for her," and then hangs up the phone. That's nice. At least he said he'd pray for her. Prayers are good. But wouldn't it mean so much more if he said, "Okay, I need to finish something here and then I'll meet you at the hospital and anoint her," and then he arranged to meet you in the emergency room lobby?

Wouldn't it be so much more comforting to have your pastor (or the hospital chaplain) actually come and see your grandma in her hospital bed, pray with her, lay his hands on her head, and then anoint her forehead and hands with oil? You bet it would. And that's the point. Like all of the Sacraments, the Anointing of the Sick is an embodied prayer, and it offers grace through stuff: through the priest, through the laying on of hands, through the oil, and in and through the community of believers.

After much thought, conversation, prayer, and study, Jen and Frank decided to live as a married couple according to the Church's teaching on marriage. That meant renouncing contraception and embracing a natural form of spacing and delaying pregnancy known as Natural Family Planning (NFP). They found that NFP actually made their marriage stronger, happier, and healthier. Not only that, their prayer led them to decide to try and conceive another child, and they are now blessed with six children.

In 2012, I had major surgery on my left knee. Because my mom was deceased, my elderly dad was legally blind, and my brother had two very young children, I needed to find a place to recover after surgery. I needed a family. So I called Jen and Frank and asked them if I could recover at their house for two to three weeks. They said yes, and the family offered me great love, comfort, support, care, and friendship—all eight of them. There's always room for another in their home and at their table.

Many of my former teens from my first parish assignment looked up to Jen and Frank as a model for marriage. Today many of them live according to the Church's teaching on marriage and family and practice NFP. As a priest, I realize that many people still disagree with the Church's stance on birth control. When I get in a discussion with such people, I rarely point to *Humanae Vitae*. I point to Jen and Frank and those other young, faithful, joyful couples who embody the teaching of the encyclical, who make the teaching incarnate. (I'm not saying that following Church teaching is easy, because it's not. I am saying that it's possible. I've seen it with my own eyes.) If reading abstract teachings in an encyclical won't convince someone of truth, perhaps a loving, warm, kind, Catholic family will.

There is nothing abstract about Jesus, just as there is nothing abstract about the Sacraments or the Catholic Church. Matter matters, and God continues to use matter to offer us his love, his forgiveness, his healing, his grace, and his Son. And because matter matters, Catholicism is never simply spiritual—it is always incarnational. Jen and Frank showed that to me.

4

Everybody Counts and Everyone Matters

The Human Person

"Amen, I say to you, whatever you did for one of these least brothers of mine, you did for me."

— *Matthew 25:40*

"If we ignore the poor, we will go to hell."

— *Archbishop Charles Chaput*

PEOPLE OFTEN ASK ME, "What's the coolest thing you've ever done as a priest?" It's a hard question to answer because as a priest I've done a lot of cool things. I imagine that all priests have, as that's the nature of the priesthood. Priests are present at the most important times of people's lives: births, deaths, marriages, family crises, sickness, celebrations, and all kinds of emergencies. And I think the coolest thing that I've ever done as a priest might have been during one of those emergency situations.

I was in my second year of priesthood the night the call came to the rectory. A parishioner had delivered her baby more than ten weeks early and she and her husband weren't sure their baby would survive, as he only weighed a few ounces over a pound. Mom and Dad asked that I come to the hospital right away to baptize their newborn son. So, I jumped in my car and drove to the hospital.

Grateful for clergy parking, I pulled into a very close spot and hustled up to the NICU. Dad met me there and filled me in about his son's dire condition, while at the same time thanking me for making the trip. He told me that before we went into the unit to see his son we would both need to scrub down. We stood next to each other at imposing stainless steel sinks for a few minutes, scrubbing our fingers, hands, and arms (all the way up to the elbow) before putting on scrubs, shower caps, face masks, and gloves.

Mom saw us right away as we made our way toward the incubator and she waved us toward her and her newborn son, who was the smallest human being I had ever seen. I had baptized adults and infants before, but a premature baby in an incubator was new to me. We were not permitted to remove the baby from the incubator, so we had to get creative.

For a valid Baptism, one must baptize with the Trinitarian formula—"I baptize you in the name of the Father, and of the Son, and of the Holy Spirit"—and use water, which has to touch the body of the one being baptized. Now, I knew the words of Baptism, but figuring out how to get water on the baby was another story. I asked the nurse if she could help me. In a minute or two, the nurse handed me a little medicine dropper filled with purified water. I pushed my gloved hands through the holes of the incubator, squeezed three perfect drops of water on to the baby's little head, and baptized him. It took less than ten seconds.

I left the hospital that night not knowing if that newly baptized baby would ever make it home. And I thought how fragile his little life was, and how his mom and dad loved him so much, even though there wasn't much there to love—less than two pounds. But he mattered. His parents knew it, and the doctors knew it, and the nurses knew it, and I knew it. In the Catholic worldview, everybody counts and everyone matters.

We are human beings, not human doings. *That we are* is more important than *what we do*. That doesn't mean what we do is unimportant, but it does mean that *being* is always prior to *doing*. You can't do anything unless you first exist. It is the Catholic belief that every human being—regardless of one's ability to do anything—matters. Every human life is sacred. Everyone counts.

We live in a culture that tends to define people by where they live, how much they make, what their bodies look like, what kind of clothes they wear, and what kind of work they do (or don't do). Defining people in this way is as old as original sin. It's nothing new. But what Judaism brought to the cultural scene, and what Christianity confirmed in the incarnation, is that every human life is sacred, as every human life is created in the image and likeness of God, regardless of age or so-called "quality" of life.

Think of the kind of people that we typically elevate as heroes in our culture. As I write this book I live in Cleveland, Ohio, where the best basketball player in the world, LeBron James, played for most of his career. James is six feet eight inches tall, weighs 250 pounds, and he regularly destroys all competition on the basketball court. He's the GOAT. He's a "bad man." And he's the King. Of course, he's also a human being, and many sports commentators argue that he's one of our finest specimens. Turning to the opposite sex, we find the goddess-like figure of Taylor Swift. Swift is tall, thin, blonde, beautiful, and musically gifted. For years she owned the country music market and then made a very successful transition to pop music. She continues to be one of the most successful recording artists in the world. Needless to say, both James and Swift are rich, powerful, beautiful, and popular. They are quintessential celebrities.

The word *celebrity* comes from the Latin *celebrare*, which means "to honor." In our culture we tend to honor those who are rich, powerful, beautiful, and famous. Catholicism also honors the rich, powerful, beautiful, and famous, not because of their riches, power, beauty, or fame, but because they are human beings made in the image and likeness of God. Catholicism also honors the poor, the weak, the unattractive, and the marginalized. Why? Because they too are human beings. In a sense, every human being is a celebrity in the Catholic worldview, because every human life matters.

Think back to the story of the Good Samaritan. Jesus tells the story while conversing with a scholar of the law about inheriting eternal life. The scholar asks Jesus, "Teacher, what must I do to inherit eternal life?" Jesus says to him, "What is written in the law? How do you read it?" So the scholar says, "You shall love the Lord, your God with all your heart, with all your being, with all your strength, and with all your mind, and your neighbor as yourself." Jesus then affirms his answer. But then the scholar says, "And who is my neighbor?" Rather than answering the question straightforwardly, Jesus tells the following story:

> "A man fell victim to robbers as he went down from Jerusalem to Jericho. They stripped and beat him and went off leaving him half-dead. A priest happened to be going down that road, but when he saw him, he passed by on the opposite side. Likewise a Levite came to the place, and when he saw him, he passed by on the opposite side. But a Samaritan traveler who came upon him was moved with compassion at the sight. He approached the victim, poured oil and wine over his wounds and bandaged them. Then he lifted him up on his own animal, took him to an inn and cared for him. The next day he took out two silver coins and gave them to the innkeeper with the instruction, 'Take care of him. If you spend more than what I have given you, I shall repay you on my way back.' Which of these three, in your opinion, was neighbor to the robbers' victim?" He answered, "The one who treated him with mercy." Jesus said to him, "Go and do likewise." (Lk 10:30–37)

At the heart of Christ's teaching is this principle: each and every human being is made in God's image and likeness, therefore each and every human being is our neighbor. Our neighbors are not just those we like, or those who are part of our family, or group, or race, or village, or country, or economic class, or even our religious or faith community. Human life is human life. And it's all sacred. Everybody counts and everyone matters.

Catholicism is especially protective of human life at its most vulnerable stages. As fallen human beings, it's easy to succumb to thinking that the dignity of the human person is found primarily in what a person does rather than in the fact that a person *is*. You may have heard it said that Catholics protect life from the moment of conception until natural death. Most people know that Catholics take a very strong and unbending stance against abortion and euthanasia and have done so for two thousand years. The reason is quite simple: human life is sacred, at every stage. From the moment of conception new human life exists, and, given the right environment, it is impossible for that life to grow into anything other than a human being. It's not just tissue, and it won't grow into a dog or become a chisel or a block of cheese. That life has a nature, and the nature is human. Science confirms it. A fetus, therefore, is not a potential human being but a human being with potential. And because all human life is created in God's image and likeness, we are charged with protecting it, defending it, and honoring it, even if it can't really do anything but grow in the womb.

In addition to protecting and honoring life at its earliest stages, Catholicism is also serious about protecting and honoring life at its last stages. Earlier in Chapter 2 I mentioned that my mom battled cancer for a good part of her life. Her cancer went into remission three times, but once it got to her liver, the chemo stopped working. She wanted to spend her final days at Holy Family Home in Parma, Ohio—a cancer home run by the Dominican Sisters of Hawthorne.[1] My mom was given from two weeks to two months to live, but in the wonderful care of the sisters, she lived for fifty-three weeks. I was with her the night before she died. As far as I know, I was the last one to speak with her.

Early the next morning, our home phone rang and the sisters invited us to be with my mom, as she was in her last hour. My dad, my brother, my pastor, the sisters, and I were all around my mom's bed when she took her final breath. It was beautiful. Yes, she suffered. But she died naturally, and she died with dignity. If you've ever been around a loved one at the moment of death, you know that you've been on holy ground.

Now, what I'm going to say next may sound shocking, but I want to say it. I need to say it. I mentioned that I was with my mom the night before she died. I knew she was dying, and I knew her death was close. If I wanted to, I could have taken a pillow and covered her face and "helped her die." I never thought of doing it, but after she died I did spend a lot of time thinking about the difference between letting death come naturally and "helping" someone die. There's a huge difference, and Catholicism recognizes that difference. My mom was in a cancer home and we all knew that she was going there to die. But keeping someone comfortable as she prepares for death is a different human act than deliberately taking the life of a person who is actively dying, or helping someone take her own life. Catholicism takes this distinction seriously and sees the first act as honoring human life and the second as an offense to it. There is a difference between someone dying naturally and directly killing someone. My mom couldn't do much of anything in her last days, but that fact did not make her life less valuable than mine. In the Catholic way of thinking, every life counts.

For Catholics, all life matters. We pay special attention to the most vulnerable stages of human life, as we often speak of "conception to natural death." But Catholicism is also very concerned with the in-between stages of life. Some of the hardest people to love are the mentally ill, the annoying, the greedy, the proud, the misinformed, and the self-righteous. Dorothy Day, Catholic activist and great friend of the poor, reportedly stated, "There are two things you need to know about the poor: they tend to smell, and they are ungrateful." Yet every life counts, so wherever there is a tendency to diminish the value of human life, we need to be there. Let's turn to the famous passage from Matthew's Gospel on the final judgment to see why:

> When the Son of Man comes in his glory, and all the angels with him, he will sit upon his glorious throne, and all the nations will be assembled before him. And he will separate them one from another, as a shepherd separates the sheep from the goats. He will place the sheep on his right and the goats on his left. Then the king will say to those on his right, "Come, you who are blessed by my Father. Inherit the kingdom prepared for you from the foundation of the world. For I was hungry and you gave me food, I was thirsty and you gave me drink, a stranger and you welcomed me, naked and you clothed me, ill and you cared for me, in prison and you visited me." Then the righteous will answer him and say, "Lord, when did we see you hungry and feed you, or thirsty and give you drink? When did we see you a stranger and welcome you, or naked and clothe you? When did we see you ill or in prison, and visit you?" And the king will say to them in reply, "Amen, I say to you, whatever you did for one of these least brothers of mine, you did for me." Then he will say to those on his left, "Depart from me, you accursed, into the eternal fire prepared for the devil and his angels. For I was hungry and you gave me no food, I was thirsty and you gave me no drink, a stranger and you gave me no welcome, naked and you gave me no clothing, ill and in prison, and you did not care for me." Then they will answer and say, "Lord, when did we see you hungry or thirsty or a stranger or naked or ill or in prison, and not

minister to your needs?" He will answer them, "Amen, I say to you, what you did not do for one of these least ones, you did not do for me." And these will go off to eternal punishment, but the righteous to eternal life. (Mt 25:31–46)

The celebrities of the Gospel look much different than LeBron James and Taylor Swift. Unlike our culture's celebrities who are set apart by their beauty, strength, wealth, power, athletic ability, musical gifts, and popularity, the celebrities identified by Jesus are the hungry, the thirsty, the stranger, the naked, the ill, the imprisoned, and those who meet their needs. It's a bizarre turn of events. To really understand the radical nature of the true celebrities of the Gospel, perhaps we ought to imagine what the red carpet at an awards ceremony would look like with the homeless and disabled making their way past the paparazzi. Would anyone really want to take pictures of the mentally ill, or those starving in worn-torn regimes, or an elderly person in a wheelchair? Or how about the pregnant teenager, or the adult with Down syndrome, or the man dying of AIDS? If we're honest with ourselves, we'll have to admit that we enjoy seeing healthy, beautiful, strong, confident people on the covers of magazines, movie screens, and on television shows. No one follows the homeless man on social media. No one has a poster of an incontinent octogenarian on her bedroom wall.

But according to the Catholic way of thinking, everybody counts and everyone matters. In God's eyes, every human life is sacred. Jesus teaches us that to truly follow him is to truly find him in the least of our brothers and sisters. He assures us that how we treat the least of our brothers and sisters determines how we spend eternity, because how we treat the least of our brothers and sisters speaks directly to our relationship with God.

Jesus' teaching in Matthew 25 is the basis for what Catholics call the Corporal Works of Mercy. They are not suggestions or recommendations. When we die, the Lord himself teaches that we will be judged on how we loved him as gauged by how we loved others. He offers seven specific acts, and each act matters: feed the hungry, give drink to the thirsty, clothe the naked, shelter the homeless, visit the sick, visit the imprisoned, and bury the dead. If you ever feel far from God or find yourself in a period of dryness in your prayer, go do a Corporal Work of Mercy. Meet Christ in the least of your brothers and sisters. Remember, Catholicism is an Incarnate faith. Doing things with your body matters. Doing the right kinds of acts with our bodies matters.

It's also worth noting that, as good as it is to support charities and institutions that do the Corporal Works of Mercy, financial support isn't the same as encountering one of Jesus' celebrities face to face. The personal encounter with one who is hungry, thirsty, naked, homeless, sick, imprisoned, or bereaved is an important one. Jesus teaches that when you encounter one of his least ones with an act of mercy, you encounter him. So visits to a nursing home, hospital, or a jail are important. Volunteering at a crisis pregnancy center, a soup kitchen, or hospice are true acts of mercy. Why? Because mercy is a gift. It's never earned. It's given freely. Just as the Father freely gave the gift of his Son to us, and just as the Son freely gave the gift of himself back to the Father for our sake, so too are we called to empty ourselves in self-giving love on account of others.

Did you know that orphanages, hospitals, and hospices as we know them today were all invented by the Catholic Church? Did you know that many religious communities of women and men have embraced lives of poverty, chastity, and obedience so that the least of their brothers and sisters could receive their love, care, respect, comfort, and dignity when no one else was willing to offer it? It's true.

One of my very favorite stories about the way in which Catholicism understands just how much everybody counts and everyone matters goes all the way back to the third century. Saint Lawrence was in charge of the treasury of the church in Rome and, as Saint Ambrose tells the story, he was instructed by the government prefect to hand over the treasures of the church. So Lawrence asked for some time to gather up the church's treasures. First, Lawrence went about distributing the church's wealth to the poor. Then, in a brilliant move, when he came back before the government officials, he brought with him the poor, the widows, the lame, the blind, and the deaf, and he said, "Here are the treasures of the Church!" He was martyred immediately. Why did he do what he did? Because Lawrence knew that everybody counted and that everyone mattered, even if it meant losing his life for the sake of promoting and protecting the dignity of the lives of others, especially the lives of the most vulnerable—God's celebrities.

At the beginning of this chapter I shared one of my favorite stories of priesthood—the time I baptized a premature baby in the NICU with a medicine dropper. The story gets better. The baby survived, and a few months after the Baptism, his parents brought him to church on a Sunday afternoon where I performed the *Rite of Bringing a Baptized Child to the Church*. Since he was already baptized in the hospital, there was no need to baptize him again, as Baptism is not repeated. However, since other rituals take place at an ordinary Baptism, those rituals were performed—the anointing with chrism, clothing with a white garment, and the presentation of a lighted candle.

A beautiful thing about Catholicism is that those baptismal symbols—water, white garment, and candle—are reintroduced at a Catholic funeral Mass. Baptism is the sacrament that washes away original sin, giving us new life and bringing us into God's family, the Church. In the Catholic funeral liturgy, when the casket is brought into the church, the priest sprinkles the casket with holy water. Then the casket is draped in a white cloth—recalling the baptismal garment. During the funeral liturgy, the casket remains at the foot of the altar next to the Paschal candle, which symbolizes the Light of Christ, first received on the day of Baptism. The symbols that were present when one came into the Church at Baptism are the same symbols present at one's death, when we pray that the deceased may inherit eternal life in Christ.

Everybody counts and everyone matters. This principle even holds in the rite of Baptism and the rite of a funeral Mass. We don't have different prayers at Baptism for someone who is rich, or strong, or beautiful, or famous. Royalty and the poor hear the same prayers, receive the same Sacraments, and are offered the same grace. A funeral Mass for a pope and a pauper are almost indistinguishable.

When Dorothy Day was in the process of her conversion and began attending Mass regularly, she was moved by the way the congregation gathered for liturgy. Bishop Robert Barron explains: "The usual societal distinctions, she noticed, were blurred, as rich and poor, educated and ignorant, members of establishment families and immigrants all came together in the same place for the same purpose." [2] What Dorothy Day noticed about the Mass is an embodiment of Catholicism itself—everybody counts and everyone matters. Would you have it any other way?

5

Show and Tell

Exemplarity

"Be imitators of me, as I am of Christ."

— *1 Corinthians 11:1*

"Modern man listens more willingly to witnesses than to teachers, and if he does listen to teachers, it is because they are witnesses."

— *Paul VI*

WHEN I WAS GROWING UP, it seemed that every priest I knew smoked cigarettes. At Saint Wendelin, the kindly Father Lajak would smoke as he walked from the rectory to the sacristy for the eleven o'clock Mass every Sunday morning. My brother and I were altar servers, and we took turns holding the Roman

Missal at the beginning and end of Mass at the cue, "*Let us pray.*" Then we both noticed not only his smoky breath but also that the page edges of the Missal had yellowish marks from his nicotine-stained fingers.

At Incarnate Word Academy, I would regularly serve the 6:30 AM daily Mass for the sisters in the convent chapel. Father Basil was a Benedictine monk who lived on the convent grounds in an old house on the corner of campus. It was often still dark as we servers waited at the convent door for Father Basil to arrive and let us in. We used to play a game to see who could spot Father Basil first, his black Benedictine habit worked like camouflage in the darkness before dawn. The first to see the little orange dot would win, and, of course, the orange dot was the burning end of his cigarette—a light in the darkness.

Father Krizner was the chaplain at Holy Name High School, and he, too, was a smoker. He wasn't showy about it, but like Father Lajak and Father Basil, we all knew that he smoked. But it never bothered any of us. After all, I was in high school in the early 90s, and smoking didn't have the taboo back then as it does today. We all knew that if we couldn't find Father Krizner in his office, or if he stepped away from retreat for a few minutes, he was likely enjoying a cigarette.

Holy Name High School was sending lots of young men to our diocesan seminary during those years, thanks to the great work of Father Krizner and his campus ministry. I distinctly remember that when those seminarians came back to visit Holy Name, they would often be seen smoking a cigarette with Father Krizner before or after one of our gatherings. It wasn't a scandal. That's just how it was. Priests smoked. Those studying to be priests also smoked. You have to start somewhere.

In the very late summer of 1994, I scrapped my college plans and decided I wanted to enter our diocesan seminary. I remember driving to Holy Name on a Sunday night in late July to tell Father Krizner about my decision. As a matter of fact, he may have been the first person I told. It was the night of our summer cookout, and teens were all over the place enjoying burgers, hot dogs, watermelon, and good Catholic fellowship. I approached Father Krizner and asked if I could speak with him privately. He obliged. We walked off to the perimeter of the parking lot and he lit a cigarette. I said, "I want to go to Borromeo next year. I think God might be calling me to be a priest." He took a drag off his smoke and sternly spoke: "You better not be bullshitting me." "I'm not. I'm serious! I think I might be called to the priesthood," I said. He exhaled a white plume of smoke just to the side of my face and calmly said, "Good. That's good." Two days later he drove me to the seminary for my admission interviews.

We human beings first come to know things through our senses. Think of a toddler who is constantly touching things, picking things up, shaking and even tasting them. When my niece was young, she used to love to play with my keys. She liked the way they felt in her hands, the sound they made as they jingled, and from time to time she would even taste them, much to her parents' chagrin. We might take it for granted that young children engage in such play, but what looks like play is actually profound learning—coming to know the world—because knowledge begins with the senses. Taste, touch, smell, sound, and especially sight give us access to the world. That is why when God sent his Son into the world, he took on flesh so that he could be encountered through the senses and, therefore, be known.

The Second Person of the Trinity is the *Logos*, the Word of God. In the incarnation, this Word becomes embodied, this Word becomes enfleshed. Why? Because we human beings learn best not by being told, but by being shown. It's one thing to tell someone about what God is like and an entirely different thing for God to become a human being and show us what God is like and what human beings should be like, just as it's one thing to read a book about how to throw a baseball and another thing to teach someone how to throw a baseball by actually playing catch with him. We learn best not by following what someone says but by watching what someone does, by actually acting with another person. It's not that words aren't important, for truly they are. It's that actions speak louder than words or, better yet, embodied words speak louder than abstract ones.

Throughout the Gospels, Jesus Christ shows us who God is, because Jesus Christ is God. He is one with the Father, so when we see Jesus, we see the Father. Not only is Jesus true God, he is also true man. Jesus shows us who God is and who we are, and he shows us both at the same time. And he does all of this with and through a human body, a body like yours and like mine.

Jesus Christ is not only the Incarnate Word; we can also call him the Incarnate Law, as he embodies and fulfills the Law given to us through Moses. Think of the Ten Commandments (see Ex 20:2–17), and then think of Jesus. With his very life he embodies each and every commandment.

1. *I, the* L<small>ORD</small>*, am your God . . . You shall not have other gods beside me.*

    Jesus loves the Father above all things and is one with the Father (see Jn 10:30).

2. *You shall not invoke the name of the* L<small>ORD</small>*, your God, in vain.*

    Jesus honors God's holy name and actually teaches us to call God *Abba*, which is more like "dad" than the formal "father" (see Mt 6:9).

3. *Remember the sabbath day—keep it holy.*

    Jesus keeps holy the Sabbath and reminds his hearers that he is the Lord of the Sabbath (see Mt 12:8).

4. *Honor your father and your mother, that you may have a long life in the land the* L<small>ORD</small> *your God is giving you.*

    Jesus honors Mary, his mother, and Joseph, his stepfather (see Lk 2:51).

5. *You shall not kill.*

    Jesus takes no life—he gives and restores life (see Jn 11:43–44).

6. *You shall not commit adultery.*

    Jesus' gaze, friendships, and actions are nothing but pure (see Jn 3:29).

7. *You shall not steal.*

    Jesus steals nothing but souls from the devil's grasp (see Mk 5:8).

8. *You shall not bear false witness against your neighbor.*

    Jesus is the Truth (see Jn 14:6).

9. You shall not covet your neighbor's house.

> Jesus is only concerned with his Father's house (see Mk 11:17).

10. You shall not covet your neighbor's wife.

> Jesus covets nothing because his life is always directed toward giving, not taking. The only thing Jesus wants to take away is the sin of the world (see Jn 1:29).

Jesus not only invites us to follow and embody the commandments, he also offers us the Beatitudes (see Mt 5:3–12) as a way of living and loving. And just as he embodied each and every commandment in his own person, he does the same with each and every beatitude. Admittedly, the Beatitudes seem strange at first glance—they're counterintuitive. To my mind, the only way to really understand the Beatitudes is to first realize that Jesus gave flesh to each of them. Contemplating that incarnate mystery is the starting point to understanding the mystery of the Beatitudes.

1. Blessed are the poor in spirit, for theirs is the kingdom of heaven.

> "My soul is sorrowful even to death" (Mt 26:38).

2. Blessed are they who mourn, for they will be comforted.

> "And Jesus wept" (Jn 11:35).

3. Blessed are the meek, for they will inherit the land.

> "He emptied himself, taking the form of a slave, coming in human likeness" (Phil 2:7).

4. Blessed are they who hunger and thirst for righteousness, for they will be satisfied.

"Woe to you scribes and Pharisees, you hypocrites. You lock the kingdom of heaven before human beings" (Mt 23:13).

5. *Blessed are the merciful, for they will be shown mercy.*

"Neither do I condemn you" (Jn 8:11).

6. *Blessed are the clean of heart, for they will see God.*

"Take it; this is my body" (Mk 14:22).

7. *Blessed are the peacemakers, for they will be called children of God.*

"Peace be with you" (Lk 24:36).

8. *Blessed are they who are persecuted for the sake of righteousness, for theirs is the kingdom of heaven.*

"If I have spoken wrongly, testify to the wrong; but if I have spoken rightly, why do you strike me?" (Jn 18:23).

9. *Blessed are you when they insult you and persecute you and utter every kind of evil against you [falsely] because of me. Rejoice and be glad, for your reward will be great in heaven. Thus they persecuted the prophets who were before you.*

"Those passing by reviled him, shaking their heads and saying, 'Aha! You who would destroy the temple and rebuild it in three days, save yourself by coming down from the cross'" (Mk 15:29–30).

In his own flesh, Jesus shows us—not just tells us—what God is like, and what humanity looks like when it is united with God. Remember that Jesus is like us in all things but sin, so the fact that he shows us how to live, to love, to pray, to surrender, to give, to receive, to heal, to teach, to preach, to rejoice, to weep, to trust, to comfort, to console, to challenge, to forgive—with and through his human body is all for our sake. Through his life he shows us what is possible for our own lives. He brings God close to us in his very self so that we can see up close what God looks like and what we look like when we live in him.

In his first encyclical, *Deus Caritas Est*, Pope Benedict XVI wrote the following: "Being a Christian is not the result of an ethical choice or a lofty idea, but the encounter with an event, a person, which gives life a new horizon and a decisive direction."[1] People often forget that Christianity is ultimately about a person. And the point of Christianity is that when we come to encounter the person of Jesus Christ, our lives change and we become like him—or better yet, we become him. By Baptism, a person is literally given a new identity as a son or daughter of the Father, and the relationship that Jesus, the Son, has with God, the Father, is then given to the baptized person by the power of the Holy Spirit. When a Christian takes this new identity seriously and embodies this new relationship, that Christian becomes a saint. And sainthood is the call of every baptized Christian.

Saints are real. Saints are attractive. They are attractive because they present the person of Jesus Christ not simply in word, but truly in action. Saints are other Christs. When you meet a saint, you meet Christ. And because a saint is a sinner who knows that he or she is loved by God, a saint also gives us hope that we, too, can become saints if we allow God to take full control of our lives.

There are thousands upon thousands of saints that offer Christian inspiration and witness, but I want to focus on three in particular: Saint Peter, Saint Monica, and Saint Augustine. I want to highlight these three saints because they have what the philosopher Max Scheler described as the phenomenon of the *zug*.[2] Scheler argues that a holy person draws others toward him or her by his or her very person. Peter, Monica, and Augustine have all drawn me close to them with their unique *zug*, and if you don't yet know their stories, my guess is that they may have a similar effect on you.

Peter

Most people know that Peter was the first pope. But we often forget that the first pope had a pretty embarrassing past. I can think of at least five times he failed terribly in his discipleship. The first time was when he was out fishing with Jesus and couldn't catch a thing (see Lk 5:1–11). Jesus commanded him to drop his nets into the deep water. (You get the sense that Peter the fisherman didn't have much confidence in the advice of Jesus the carpenter.) Peter reluctantly obliged. That night he had the biggest catch of his life and knelt before Jesus saying, "Depart from me, Lord, for I am a sinful man" (5:8). The second time was that night when Jesus walked on water to the disciples on the boat (see Mt 14:22–33). Peter began to walk on water, but the strong wind frightened him and he began to sink. Jesus rescued him and said, "O you of little faith, why did you doubt?" (14:31). The third time was when Jesus was predicting his passion to Peter and the other disciples. When Peter objected, Jesus told him, "Get behind me, Satan!" (16:23). The fourth time was at the Last Supper, when Jesus was washing the feet of his Apostles. Peter first refused to have his feet washed, then asked Jesus to wash all of him (see Jn 13:8–9). The fifth time was the worst, when Peter denied knowing Jesus on the night before he died (see Lk 22:54–62). Peter was standing around a charcoal fire when he denied knowing Jesus not once, not twice, but three times. It's the worst sin someone could commit. Remember that the number three is a perfect number, biblically speaking, so the fact that Peter denied Jesus three times has a sense of finality to it.

Peter is you and me. We need to see ourselves in Peter. He wants to do right and love and serve the Lord, but he fails time and again. So what does the Lord do with Peter? The same thing that he does with us: he meets us in our brokenness and offers us his mercy, forgiveness, and healing. He desires to re-create us, which is exactly what Jesus did for Peter next to another charcoal fire on the beach after his resurrection. Jesus knows that Peter denied him three times the night before he died, but he never stops loving Peter; he offers Peter another chance. He asks Peter three times if he loves him. And each time Peter says, "Yes, Lord, you know that I love you." In that encounter, Jesus recreates Peter through his mercy and forgiveness. And in time Peter literally becomes another Christ when he becomes a saint.

The Acts of the Apostles immediately follows the four Gospels in the Bible, and the title of the book is self-explanatory. In their encounter with the risen Lord, Peter and the other Apostles become other Christs, and this fifth book in the New Testament tells us about the Apostles' actions. Peter and the Apostles, having been recreated by the Risen Lord, go about preaching, teaching, and healing, just as Jesus did. They also experience persecution, just as Jesus did. And they also die, just as Jesus did. But they were willing to die, because they believed that Christ's death conquered death, and that in the resurrection death had no more power over them.

If you make your way to Rome today, or even if you watch some papal event on television, keep this in mind when you see Saint Peter's Basilica. That church, the largest Catholic church in the world, is literally built upon the bones of a sinful man who doubted Jesus, who couldn't walk on water, who attempted to correct Jesus, who didn't want Jesus to wash his feet, and who denied knowing Jesus three times when our Lord needed him most. Peter was a sinner. But the Lord met Peter in his sinfulness and recreated him. Peter trusted that the mercy of Jesus was greater than any of his sins, and he allowed the Lord to make him a saint. If Jesus can make a guy like Peter a saint, what might he do with you?

Monica

Saint Monica is a favorite saint of mothers who are worried about their children, especially their adult children. As a parish priest, I would often direct mothers to Saint Monica when they came to me with concerns about children who were drifting from the faith or who crashed into the rocks of life's shore. Monica was Saint Augustine's mother, and she prayed for him ceaselessly.

Most people don't know that when Saint Monica was younger, she had a drinking problem.[3] Her parents would regularly send young Monica to fetch some wine out of the cask in the family home. But before Monica poured the wine into her parents' pitcher, she would take a little sip for herself. In time, those little sips increased, and before long Monica fell into the habit of drinking cups full of wine. But one day one of the maidservants insulted Monica harshly, calling her a "winebibber," and she stopped for good. (It's a good lesson in speaking the truth in charity. If you don't have friends who speak the truth to you, then you don't have friends at all.)

I like Monica's story because few people know that, at one time in her life, Monica had real struggles. She, too, was a sinner. But the Lord met her where she was and transformed her life. Then he sent her to be another Christ and help transform the life of her son Augustine.

How many mothers today struggle with anxiety about their children, yet think themselves powerless in offering any real help? How many moms, like Monica, have shed tears, lost sleep, gained wrinkles and grey hairs over concern for the fruit of their wombs? That's Monica's story too. And her story didn't end in tragedy, but in glory.

Augustine

Saint Augustine is one of the brightest lights in the Christian tradition. But he wasn't always a saint. Augustine had major struggles with lust. Although his story is often told as if he were a player, he wasn't necessarily promiscuous, but he was unchaste. Augustine fathered a child out of wedlock. When he broke up with the mother of his child, he wrote, "I was not so much a lover of marriage as a slave to lust; I procured another woman, but not, of course, my wife."[4] At one point, when part of him really desired to live a life of purity and another part of him wanted to cling to sexual pleasure, he prayed this prayer: "Give me chastity and continence, but not yet!"[5]

Monica prayed for Augustine daily, and just by living her life (of prayer, fasting, almsgiving, devotion, etc.), she was his witness of discipleship. Along the way, Augustine met Saint Ambrose, the bishop of Milan, who also showed Augustine what holiness, discipleship, and Christian freedom looked like in the flesh. Inspired by these witnesses, and encountering the person of Jesus in these saints, Augustine eventually entered into relationship with the Lord, was baptized, and became a saint himself.

Perhaps the greatest thing about Augustine's story is that he shares it with us. In his book *Confessions*, he tells his conversion story and he doesn't whitewash anything. He lets us in on his struggles with pride, disobedience, and especially lust. And here's the most shocking part of all: he published *Confessions* while he was a bishop! Imagine the bishop of your diocese writing a book detailing his own sinful past and then documenting his conversion into the life of grace. It wouldn't happen. But it happened in the fifth century, and it happened because Augustine wanted his flock to know that the transformation he experienced in his life was possible for everyone, regardless of their past. Augustine wrote the *Confessions* to inspire others to become saints. And how refreshing it is to read about a saint's struggles with impurity, knowing that by God's grace such struggles can be overcome.

Saint Peter, Saint Monica, and Saint Augustine don't just tell us what holiness and authentic Christian living are about, they show us. Just as Jesus didn't simply tell us about the Commandments or the Beatitudes, but showed us how they are lived with his very life, the saints also show us how to be other Christs by their own lives. Catholicism is a very sensual faith, and it has to be, because we first come to knowledge through our senses. Saints show us what it looks like to transform from a life of sin to a life of grace. They show us that holiness is possible for everyone. They glorify the Lord by their lives so that we may do the same with ours.

In my first week at college seminary, I bought a carton of cigarettes and decided that I would become a smoker. All the priests I knew growing up smoked, and I figured there was no better time to start. I was a heavy smoker during my freshman year and then quit for a while before picking it up again socially during my junior year. I was a social smoker for the rest of my time in the seminary, smoking a little over a pack a week.

After ordination I was sent to my first parish. I didn't want to be a bad example for my young parishioners, so I became a closet smoker. I would smoke from the balcony in my second floor room in the rectory. (Truth be told, I used to flick my cigarette butts into the gutter on the pastor's roof, until one day he complained to me that the high school kids must have been smoking on his roof.) When I was studying at the Catholic University of America (CUA) I continued to smoke, but never in my collar and mostly by myself.

I had my last cigarette on May 31, 2009. I quit for three reasons. First, penance. Second, I was running a lot of road races at the time and figured that you can't be both a good smoker and a good runner. One of them had to go. Third, I would start my new job as a seminary formator that fall and I knew the power of example. I would be the new young priest on the faculty, and I knew from being a seminarian that, for better or for worse, seminarians follow the example of their priestly formators. I didn't want any seminarians to start or continue to smoke because of me. I have other bad habits, but by the grace of God, smoking is no longer one of them. And if God could help free me from that bad habit, I'm hopeful that he's willing to do a lot more in me, with me, and for me in the future.

How about you? What are some habits and behaviors in your life that need to change? Where does God's grace need to be at work in your life? How is God calling you to conversion so that you too can be a saint? If you can answer those questions, you're not far from the Kingdom.

6

Take Up and Read

The Beautiful and Intelligent Life

"How beautiful you are,
      how fair,
my love, daughter of delights!"

— *Song of Songs 7:7*

"We tire easily of abstractions and crave visible signs."

— *Robert Louis Wilken*

I HAVE NEVER BEEN an excellent student, but my grades were pretty good until about the sixth grade. As a child, I liked to read and write, and I did especially well in my art classes, although I was never good at math. When my brother, Adam, and I were preparing to sell our family home, I discovered that my mom had saved most of the stories that I'd written and most of the art that I'd made during my grade school years at Incarnate Word Academy. (I wrote a book in fifth grade for Sister Elizabeth's English class about my friends and me rescuing Bruce Springsteen from Libya, where he was being held hostage.) Mom also saved my report cards. After studying them, it became very clear to me that when puberty hit, my grades took a hit. Hormones will do that to you, I guess.

High school was pretty much the same story for me. I wasn't a great student, and I blame that on a few things. First, I didn't try very hard. The most important things to me in high school were my friends and sports. I did just enough in the classroom to make sure that I could play baseball and not get grounded by my parents. Mediocrity and sloth had a hold on me. Second, like most sons, I looked up to my dad. But my dad never liked school. (I recently learned that my Grandpa Ference stopped school after third grade and my Grandma Ference after eighth, so my dad's indifference to education makes sense.) My dad was a construction worker, and the only things I ever remember him reading were the parish bulletin, the newspaper, and his *Elevator Union* journal. He often told me that an education was important, but he never said why. I think my mom must have told him to tell me that. He had a good life and a good family and a good job, but he barely had a high school degree, and so I figured an education couldn't be that important. Third, I really was bad at math. Freshman algebra was the worst and it set the tone for my high school career. Most other kids in my class would sail through their homework and their exams, but not me. I felt dumb. So I stopped trying. I figured that school wasn't my thing, and I knew a lot of people who did well in life who weren't great students (like my dad). I also knew a lot of people who did very well in school but couldn't swing a hammer or change a flat tire, so why would I want to be like them?

I took that attitude with me to Borromeo Seminary. My first year of college was pretty much the same as my four years of high school. I earned a 2.4 GPA and was pleased that I did just enough work to stay off academic probation. My prayer life was good, my social life was great, and I was really enjoying all my new friends at the seminary. School was something that I had to do. I heard a brother seminarian once say, "Cs get degrees," and I thought that was a great motto. I also remember one of the guys from our theologate explain that once you get ordained, none of your parishioners will ever ask you about your GPA. That sounded right.

At the beginning of my sophomore year of college, Father Monroe, the academic dean of the seminary, called me to his office. He told me that it appeared I was fitting nicely into the community, that the faculty liked me, that I was making good friends, that I was learning to play guitar and enjoying music in a new way, and that I was basically happy. I nodded in agreement. Then it happened. "Your grades stink," he said. "Cs get degrees," I responded. "Why don't you do yourself and the Church a big favor?" he said and took a drag of his cigarette. "If you're not going to start studying, you should leave the seminary. The last thing the Church needs are more dumb priests."

Like the rich young man in the parable, my face fell and I went away sad. I returned to my dorm room, and I don't remember for how long I sat there, but it was long enough to let Father Monroe's words sink in. Did he really think I should leave? Did he really think I was dumb? Was I really hurting the Church by not studying? Heck, I knew a lot of priests who weren't super smart but were good, holy priests. What about Saint John

Vianney? He was a terrible student. So I decided to go back to Father Monroe for some clarification. "Father Monroe, do you really think that I should leave the seminary?" I asked sheepishly. "Listen," he replied, "you're not dumb. But you are lazy. And if you're not going to study, then you're not going to have anything to give to the people of God who deserve good preaching and teaching. You've got a sharp mind. Why don't you start using it?"

And that was the start of my intellectual conversion.

Beauty, Art, Architecture, and the Human Person

The Catholic Church is smart. We also have a lot of rituals and rules. And yes, to an outsider, some of the things that we do may seem a bit strange. But as Robert Barron likes to say, the Church is like a medieval cathedral. From the outside it may look dark and daunting, but once you step into the cathedral and see the gothic arches reaching up to heaven, the light pouring in through the stained glass windows, the hand-carved wood and stone that make up altars, statues, and choir stalls, it starts to make sense. There is an order to things, and those things are telling a story. It's a good story, and it's a true story.

When God became one of us in the person of Jesus Christ, he reminded us that creation is good, that matter is good. Again, God didn't become an angel, but, by the power of the Holy Spirit, he took on flesh and became like us in all things but sin. When Jesus died, he died with a body. When Jesus rose, he rose with a body—a glorified body, but a body nonetheless. And when he ascended to the Father, he did so with his glorified body. So when early Christians started telling his story, they told it with and through their bodies—in their preaching, in their teaching, and even in their martyrdom.

Let's consider the importance of the body for a moment. As human beings, everything we do, we do with a body. That's part of what it means to be a human being. And even when we pray, it's not as if somehow our souls leave our bodies to commune with God. When we pray we actually use our bodies to unite us with God. Think of the kinds of things people do with their bodies when they pray. They fold their hands, they kneel, they put their hands on their hearts, they sit quietly with hands on their laps, they sing, they chant, they extend their hands in the ancient *orans* position, they prostrate themselves on the floor (a favorite position of Ignatius of Loyola and John Paul II), they roll beads through their fingers, they bow, they genuflect, they stand at attention, and they even write icons.

When Christians pray, we do whatever we can to enter more deeply into union with God, and that often means assisting our prayer not only with posture but also with beauty. It's very important to note that God has absolutely no need of our praise and adoration. God is God, and our failure to worship him can never make him any less than he is. If it did, he wouldn't be God, because he would then somehow depend upon his creation—which he does not. All the beautiful statues, windows, altar pieces, hand-carved reliefs, icons, frescoes, and mosaics assist us in our worship of God, but God doesn't need any of these beautiful things to be God. We human beings, however, do need such things. Think about it. Plato taught that beauty lifts us out of ourselves. So beautiful liturgical vessels help us appreciate the sacredness of the Eucharist, just as high soaring arches help us lift our hearts, minds, and hands to heaven in prayer. If we were angels, such things wouldn't be necessary, but we're not pure spirits. We have bodies as well as souls, so sacred, holy, and beautiful things matter to us. They help us come to know God and to worship him.

Remember, Aristotle and Aquinas both taught that knowledge begins with the senses. It doesn't end with them. That means that in coming to know the world, including the mysteries of faith, our senses matter. And this is precisely the principle behind the Catholic Church's love of beauty. We want our churches, chapels, oratories, and shrines to be beautiful because we want people to be able to encounter God and his love for us in those places.

Since the beginning, Christians have used art and architecture to tell the story of Jesus Christ. Recall that for much of the history of Christianity a good number of believers were illiterate, so one of the best ways to tell the story of the faith was through sign and symbol. The earliest preserved Christian art is limited to burial places, such as the catacombs.[1] Scenes from Scripture were commonly depicted on catacomb walls, and as Church historian Robert Louis Wilken notes, "With few exceptions Christian leaders welcomed paintings in the churches, and bishops praised the work of these artists."[2] Because God became one of us, it became appropriate for us to present the story of Jesus Christ in images—a distinction between Christians and other monotheists.

Good Christian art became a teacher, a storyteller. Wilken explains, "A painting gave the faithful an image to carry in the mind and served as a book for those who could not read. Over time, however, it became customary not only to look at the pictures, but also to touch them, kiss them, light candles in front of them, even address prayers to them."[3] Often, Catholics are accused of idolatry because of our practice of praying before statues, icons, and frescos. True Catholic worship is never directed to a thing, but always to the Father, through the Son, by the power of the Holy Spirit. However, because we are not pure spirits but body-persons, we use our bodies to pray. We pray by looking *through* beautiful art to be with the one depicted.

Speaking of bodies, it's important to note that the beauty of the Church is for everybody. Yes, we Catholics have some priceless pieces of art that could fetch a pretty penny if we sold them, but something many critics of the Church often forget is that the poor need beauty too. I vividly remember spending time in Rome in 2000 for World Youth Day with a group of pilgrims from my home parish. We walked through the jubilee doors hand in hand and then toured Saint Peter's Basilica and saw Michelangelo's *Pietà* and Bernini's columns. Eventually, we made our way through the Vatican museum, taking in splendid works by Raphael, Giotto, and da Vinci, and finally seeing the magnificence of the Sistine Chapel. But guess what? We weren't the only ones enjoying all of the beauty. Pilgrims from all around the world, including some very poor parts of the world, were touring these beautiful and holy places. We all appreciated the wonderful artistic treasures the Church had on display. Had the Church decided to sell these pieces and give the money to the poor, it's not very likely that the poor would ever have the opportunity to see such beauty. The Church knows that the poor also need beauty, and so the Church provides beauty to all people, even and especially the poor. If the Church is indeed the People of God, then it is right and just that the People of God possess and have access to some of the world's greatest treasures.

One of the most visited Catholic churches in the United States is the Basilica of the National Shrine of the Immaculate

Conception in Washington, D.C. I spent a lot of time there when I was studying next door at CUA. Every Third Sunday I would offer Mass in the crypt church, but mostly I'd stop in just to pray. Although some churches in the United States are more beautiful than the Basilica, the National Shrine is unique in that each side chapel—and there are many of them—is dedicated to a particular title of Mary. So, no matter your nationality, chances are you will find a side chapel with an image of Mary that looks like you.

My paternal grandparents came to the United States from Slovakia in 1910, so I used to enjoy praying before the statue of our Lady of Sorrows, the patron saint of Slovakia, in the lower level of the Basilica. (I'm told she was recently elevated to the upper church.) But I also enjoyed seeing people of all different ethnicities finding the Marian chapel dedicated to their particular people. The two most striking side chapels, in my opinion, are found on either side of the crypt church, facing north. One is dedicated to Our Mother of Africa, and to enter you have to walk over an image of a slave ship carved in the threshold tile, a vivid reminder of the suffering that so many Africans and African Americans endured. Mary is strong, beautiful, and black, and she's confidently holding Jesus in her arms. When I was studying at CUA, a man who never wore shoes would often stand in this chapel and pray for hours, and he looked like Mary's relative. I always felt blessed to see him. The other chapel that I find striking, the Vietnamese chapel, is decorated mostly in vibrant mosaic tile depicting Our Lady of La Vang in the center, the Vietnamese martyrs on the left, and Mary's apparition to the right. The striking mosaic ceiling is a deep celestial blue speckled with stars, but the chapel is most alive when Vietnamese pilgrims come to visit, which I've witnessed. Seeing an image of Our Lady that looks like you points directly to the incarnation, and connects you to God through his mother in a most beautiful and maternal way.

I realize that for the past forty or fifty years Catholic churches haven't always lived up to the standard of the long-standing tradition of beauty for which we've been known. In most dioceses in the United States, the most beautiful churches are also the oldest churches, and most of them are either way out in the country or deep in the city. Once in a while you'll find a gem in a first-ring suburb, but it's fairly rare. Sociologists have noted that you can tell a lot about a culture by its skyline. For centuries, the highest buildings in a city were the churches. What are the tallest buildings in our cities today? Do some research and you'll see that most are banks and businesses, which in themselves aren't bad. But when their cold and rigid architecture towers over our beautiful churches, it should make us think long and hard about what is most important to our culture and what ought to be. Where beauty is lacking, so is humanity, and when humanity isn't what it should be, it's for lack of God.

The Catholic Intellectual Tradition

One of the most satisfying things about Catholicism is how intelligent it is. Two of the greatest figures in our tradition who embody that intelligence are Saint Augustine (354–430) and Saint Thomas Aquinas (c. 1225–1274). Although they were separated by eight centuries, their thought has a great deal in common, and so many of our iterations and formulations about the Christian faith can be traced back to them. (Saint Augustine is the most cited saint in the *Catechism of the Catholic Church*.) Certainly, other great thinkers have enriched our tradition, such as Justin Martyr, Irenaeus, Athanasius, Basil, Jerome, Cyril,

Gregory, Anselm, Bonaventure, Teresa of Ávila, Edith Stein, Elizabeth Anscombe, Joseph Ratzinger, and Rene Girard, but for our purposes Augustine and Aquinas will do.

In Augustine's *Confessions*, the saint presents us with the story of his conversions. Often, people want to say that Augustine had one major conversion, but upon a careful read, we'll notice that he actually had three. The first conversion happened when he read Cicero's *Hortensius* and was introduced to philosophy, the love of wisdom. Up to this point in his life, Augustine had been wrapped up in himself, especially the attention, glory, and reputation that he found in being a great rhetorician. But when he began to study philosophy and realized that there was more to living than honor, his heart turned. This was his intellectual conversion. Augustine's second conversion is recounted in Book Eight of *Confessions* and is sometimes referred to as his *Tolle Lege* moment. Besides pride, the other big sin Augustine struggled with was lust. One day, he was in a garden outside of Milan and could not figure out why he thought things he didn't want to think and did things that he didn't want to do. He wanted to change his ways but he didn't know how. Just then he heard what sounded like a child saying *tolle lege* ("take up and read"). He remembered a story about Saint Anthony of the Desert basically playing Bible roulette—opening the Bible at random to find a message—so Augustine picked up Paul's Letter to the Romans and read part of the thirteenth chapter. Upon reading it, he felt released from his lustful desires. This was his moral conversion. His third conversion—his Christian conversion—came at the Easter Vigil in 387 when he was baptized at the age of thirty-two along with his son, Adeodatus, and his friend Alypius.

I mention these three conversions because Saint Augustine wasn't always a saint, but he was always bright and intellectually curious. He was known as one of the brightest lights of his time. Augustine longed for truth and for something that would satisfy him, yet all the things that the world promised would satisfy him left him wanting. When he went through his conversions —intellectual, moral, and Christian—he never abandoned his intellectual pursuits or his desire for knowledge and wisdom. Augustine found that Christian faith actually broadened his reason, it did not destroy it. For the first half of his life, Augustine had fallen in love with creation and hoped that honor, knowledge, sexual intimacy, and even friendship would satisfy his desires, but as he tells us, his heart remained restless. He found that rest only when his life was first ordered to the Creator. Then he was able to actualize his full potential as a human being and as an intellectual.

Saint Thomas Aquinas didn't have the same sordid past as Augustine, but he did recognize himself as a sinner who needed God's mercy, which is the starting point of Christianity. Monsignor Robert Sokolowski, my thesis director at CUA, liked to say that Aquinas is to philosophy what Shakespeare is to literature. There are a lot of great philosophers, but there is only one Thomas Aquinas. What makes Aquinas so special? First, he wrote more than most people will read in a lifetime. Second, he seemed to know something about everything, and he was usually right. Third, he was a master of making distinctions, which is at the heart of all good philosophy. Fourth, and perhaps most importantly, when you read Aquinas, you are also reading the history of philosophy, as Aquinas is constantly citing not only Sacred Scripture but also thinkers like Plato, Aristotle, Augustine, Anselm, Cicero, Maimonides, Averroes, and Avicenna. Note that this little litany includes not only Christian thinkers but also pagan, Jewish, and Muslim thinkers as well. Aquinas knew that truth was truth no matter where one found it.

When I teach modern philosophy to the seminarians, one of the books we read is Machiavelli's *The Prince*, which isn't considered a great Catholic work. However, to have them practice Thomistic thinking, I have the seminarians pick three good themes from Machiavelli (such as having foresight, avoiding sycophants and flattery, and picking advisors) and write a letter to their pastor encouraging him to employ these good ideas. The purpose of the paper is to show that truth shows up in strange places, and we shouldn't be afraid to use it where we find it.

If you are familiar with Bishop Barron's website *Word on Fire*, you'll note that his movie reviews are exceptionally Thomistic. Many Catholics might reject the idea that an R-rated film such as *The Departed*, *Fargo*, or *Gran Torino* could have redemptive value, but Barron always seems to find it. Why? Because his eyes are attracted to truth, even in places where many may think no truth is present. Such is the Catholic intellectual vision. It's not sheltered or locked within a fortress; it believes that God is good and that everything that God created is good. And if your vision is sharp, by the help of God's grace, faith will actually broaden your reason, not diminish it. You'll be able to see the world and all its beauty more clearly and vividly, recognizing truth wherever it presents itself.

An interesting problem is that a modern atheism emerged with the advent of modern science. That is strange since so many of the major advances in science arose from the Catholic intellectual tradition of Europe, which held that the universe is intelligible because God created it and endowed us with the intellect to come to know it and discover its laws. Many Catholics made great contributions to science. For example, did you know that a Catholic priest formulated the Big Bang theory? His name was Georges Lemaître.

One of the greatest myths of modernity is that Christianity is somehow an enemy of science and reason. John Paul II wrote a brilliant encyclical in 1998 entitled *Fides et Ratio* that systematically debunks that lie. And Pope Francis' first encyclical, *Lumen Fidei*, makes a great argument that faith isn't out to replace reason but to broaden it. (There are many proofs for God's existence based on reason alone, but revelation tells us not only *that* God exists but also *who* God is. Reason alone can show us that God exists, but only revelation can show us that God is Trinity or that God took on flesh in Jesus Christ. More on this topic in Chapter 7.)

The point is that some of the greatest thinkers of the world have been Catholic, and their Catholic faith didn't inhibit their thinking and creativity but enhanced it. My favorite example of this phenomenon is Flannery O'Connor, who continuously reminded her readers that she was the writer that she was not *in spite of* her Catholic faith but *because of it*. Ironically, when critics of the Church claim that Christian faith contradicts reason or that Catholicism opposes science, you soon learn that such critics have failed in their research, especially in the history of Western Civilization and its greatest minds.

Father Monroe, the priest who inspired my intellectual conversion, died suddenly on November 2, 1996, All Souls' Day. I was devastated. The man most responsible for my intellectual conversion was gone, and I felt abandoned. Fortunately, I retained the lessons he taught me about always reading with a dictionary, marking my books with a pen as I read, and reading often and from a variety of disciplines. I met some professors at John Carroll University—the Jesuit school in Cleveland with which Borromeo Seminary is partnered—who taught me to love etymology, literature, poetry, history, and, even more, philosophy. My grades began to improve, and not because I wanted good grades, but because I was enjoying learning and the intellectual life.

When I started at Saint Mary Seminary, our graduate seminary in Cleveland, I took a cue from Robert Pirsig's book *Zen and the Art of Motorcycle Maintenance* and decided that I would not open my report cards for the next five years. I wanted to study for wisdom and not simply for grades or to meet a seminary requirement. And that's what I did. For five years I left all my report cards sealed, and it never bothered me—I'd asked my formation advisor to let me know if there was ever any concern about my academic performance. There weren't any. But I can tell you this: there is a great freedom in not being concerned about grades and in studying for wisdom's sake.

I was a parish priest for four years after ordination. Saint Mary's Parish in Hudson, Ohio, is an affluent, well-educated parish, and although I had a lot of charges as the parochial vicar while serving there, my favorite ministry was working with and ministering to the youth of the parish. In seminary, I used to read stories and look at pictures of young Karol Wojtyla with his student friends—praying, hiking, kayaking, conversing, laughing, studying, and traveling—and I wanted to be a priest like that. So in addition to the ordinary responsibilities of our LifeTeen ministry, I brought a few teens on to my RCIA team and also brought a few teens into full communion with the Church. And I added four field trips to the RCIA schedule in order to get my catechumens and candidates out into the city to see what Catholic living looked and felt like. We'd visit the Cleveland Museum of Art, historic churches, soup kitchens, Lenten Fish Frys, and always share a meal afterward.

I also started a summer book club at the parish, figuring that parishioners would like to read some good books with their priest during the summer. We read all sorts of books by authors like C. S. Lewis, George Weigel, John Allen, Flannery O'Connor, Wendy Shalit, and Robert Barron. And I would take any teens who came to the book club out for ice cream afterward, and then we'd pray night prayer when we returned to the parish.

Why am I telling you all this? Because at my first parish I recognized that many young people are hungry to learn about the intellectual, liturgical, and cultural traditions of Catholicism. After some study at CUA, I returned to Borromeo Seminary to teach full time. After two years on faculty, I spoke with my rector and then my bishop about starting a summer institute at our seminary. We would call it {TOLLE LEGE} and we'd draw the best and brightest teens around the diocese for a week of immersion into the richness of Catholicism at our seminary. There were all sorts of summer camps for teens—basketball camp, band camp, Appalachian Service Project, Catholic Heart Work Camp, Steubenville Conferences, etc. But I saw a great lack when it came to providing exposure to the intellectual, liturgical, and cultural aspects of the Church. My bishop agreed.

In the summer of 2012, we offered our first two weeks of {TOLLE LEGE} to some brave, young Catholic nerds from the Diocese of Cleveland. Every year since then, anywhere from twenty-four to thirty-six young men and women spend a week of their summer at our seminary—learning to pray the Liturgy of the Hours; studying six hours of philosophy and six hours of theology (from seminary professors with doctorates); visiting historic churches; touring the Cleveland Museum of Art; celebrating daily Mass; sharing communal meals; learning to use technology responsibly; adoring the Lord in the Eucharist; meeting good priests, religious sisters, and married couples; reflecting theologically on films; appreciating Catholic art and architecture; laughing; singing; and experiencing Catholicism in all its glory.

If {TOLLE LEGE} had been around when I was in high school, I would not have attended. And even if I did apply, I likely would not have been accepted, as I had not yet experienced my intellectual conversion. But isn't it funny how God works? The guy who used to say "Cs get degrees," has replaced his mentor, Father Monroe, on the seminary faculty, and he now runs a nerd camp for young Catholics, handing down the intellectual treasure of the Church to the next generation. Faith broadens reason, indeed.

7

A Vivid World

The Both/And Worldview

"For when I am weak, then I am strong."

— *2 Corinthians 12:10*

"How am I a hog and me both? How am I saved and from hell too?"

— *Ruby Turpin (from Flannery O'Connor's "Revelation")*

MANY PRIESTS WANTED TO be priests when they were young. Not me. I wanted to be a rock star. In fact, in fifth grade Sister Elizabeth made us all write a book. Mine was entitled *A Ticket to Adventure*. It was about me and my closest friends rescuing Bruce Springsteen from the Libyan army. Sister

Elizabeth made us all write an About the Author page at the end of the book. Here's what I wrote for mine: "Damian Ference is a wrestler and plays basketball. He is not married yet but hopes to be in 14 years. He was born January eigth (sic) nineteen seventy sixth (sic). He is now attending IWA. He has a mom a dad and one brother. He also has a dog. He hopes to be a Rock star or a zoo keeper." The irony was that I didn't have the patience or discipline to learn to read music, let alone to play an instrument. But I could dream.

I don't know exactly what it was about rock music that stirred my young soul. Maybe it was that my dad listened to polkas and World War II era music, and my mom was into John Denver and Placido Domingo. I found energy, power, and a hunger in rock music that seemed foreign to my mom and dad and their musical tastes but resonated deep within me. Even at a young age I knew there were certain lyrics, attitudes, and values that were contrary to my Catholic faith, but I also recognized some ridiculously good musicianship, songwriting, and themes within rock music that commanded my respect and attention. There was a deep tension within my young self to try and figure out how I could be a good Catholic kid *and* want my MTV, both at the same time. I wondered if it were possible.

Right when I was hitting puberty, a new band from Los Angeles released their debut album *Appetite For Destruction*. Guns N' Roses had raw power, loads of attitude, serious talent, and a sound that I had never ever heard before. It was heavy, it was dark, but it was also really good. My best friends at Incarnate Word and I soon knew the entire record (or cassette, to be more accurate) by rote. My mom didn't like the sound, and my dad thought that all rock music sounded the same so of course he didn't like it either.

One morning, my mom surprised me when she came out of my room with my copy of *Appetite* in her hand. She said, "Look at the cover of this album. I don't like this cross with the skulls on it. I'm throwing it away." I immediately was grateful that she didn't unfold the liner notes to read the lyrics and see more of the album art, but for some reason I just said, "Mom, you can do whatever you want, but you can't stop rock 'n' roll." And my mom cried.

To this day I don't know why I said that, but I have confessed it since.

Some people like to say that the world is black and white. Surely in terms of morality there are certain things that one should never do, and the either/or has its place. But according to the Catholic perspective, the world is not black and white—it's actually full of color, like a peacock's tail. As a matter of fact, Flannery O'Connor, who owned more than forty peacocks, once described the symbolism of the eyeball pattern on the male peacock's tail as the *all-seeing eyes* of the Church. In other words, the Catholic worldview has breadth and depth—it sees unity and mystery where the eyes of the world see contradiction.

Things are easier when they are *either/or* rather than *both/ and*. But the fullness of truth and the fullness of reality is, more often than not, a both/and kind of thing. For example, many people say a big reason that they don't come to Mass on Sunday is because it's boring—the music stinks and the preaching is irrelevant. Others argue that it doesn't matter what kind or quality of music is played or what the homily is about. As long as you hear the word of God and are able to receive the Eucharist, then that should be enough. Who is right? Both are right.

It is true that if the word of God is proclaimed and the bread and wine become the Body and Blood of Christ at the consecration, then you have yourself a Mass. But it's just as true that when the music is good, and the preaching is good, and when the community—priest included—is locked-in and praying with everything they have, then the Mass becomes more efficacious. Good music and good preaching invite people to enter more deeply into the word and the Word made Flesh in the Eucharist. When the People of God and the priests of God enter into the Mass with full, active, and conscious participation (which includes silence, by the way), the Mass becomes more attractive and beautiful. It's the both/and principle at work.

In some ways, Catholicism can be understood as a huge collection of the both/and principle. In the rest of this chapter we're going to look at several different realities that are so rich and mysterious, they can only be understood through the both/and lens. It would be impossible to name all such realities, but a few are most necessary, while others are not as portentous but still remain noteworthy.

God and His Mother

The first statement of the Nicene Creed is "I believe in one God." By professing that we believe in *one God,* we are also professing that we don't believe in *many gods.* The Jews were set apart from all their neighboring communities by their belief in one God, not many. But as the Creed continues to unfold, we notice that, in addition to our belief that God is one, we also believe in the Trinity, one God in three divine Persons. The Preface for the Feast of the Most Holy Trinity puts it this way: "You are one God, one Lord: not in the unity of a single person, but in a Trinity of one substance." So God is Father, Son, and Holy Spirit, yet one God. And the *Catechism of the Catholic Church* says, "We do not confess three Gods, but one God in Three Persons" (no. 253).

Recall the moment when God presented himself to Moses in the burning bush. Scripture tells us, "Although the bush was on fire, it was not being consumed" (Ex 3:2). Note the both/and principle at work. A bush that is on fire should eventually be consumed by that very fire, but this bush was both on fire and not consumed at the same time. What's happening here is that God is showing Moses something about his nature, and he's also giving a sneak preview of the incarnation. In the person of Jesus Christ, the Second Person of the Trinity becomes human, yet remains God. The two natures of Christ are not in competition with each other, just as God is not in competition with us. Jesus Christ is true God and true man. All the Christological heresies somehow favor one over the other. Upholding Christ's divinity but denying his humanity is a heresy, just as upholding Christ's humanity and denying his divinity is a heresy. The truth is that Jesus Christ is both truly divine and truly human at the same time, and the fullness and mystery of that truth can only be understood through the both/and principle. Jesus Christ is one Person with two natures.

Another both/and reality at work in the incarnation is how we understand our relationship with God. Is God totally other, completely mysterious, and well beyond our comprehension? Or is God close at hand, accessible, intimate, and like one of us? The answer is that, in the incarnation especially, God reveals himself as both transcendent and immanent at the same time, not one or the other.

One of the most important Christological councils in the early Church took place at Ephesus in 431. One of the big issues at that council was the use of the title *Theotokos* (bearer of God) for the Virgin Mary. As you've probably guessed, the council approved the title, as we now say "Holy Mary, Mother of God" every time we pray the Hail Mary. We can call Mary Mother of God because Jesus is one Person, the Son of God. By becoming the mother of Jesus, Mary became the Mother of God, because she gave birth to him in his human nature. Although it is true to say that the Council of Ephesus was primarily a Christological council, it does remind us that Mary, too, can only be understood through the mysterious both/and reality of Catholicism, because Mary is both Virgin and Mother.

The Human Person

In the Nicene Creed, we also state that we believe that God is Creator: "maker of heaven and earth, of all things visible and invisible." As human beings, we are one of those parts of creation that have both visible and invisible qualities. Recall that the second chapter of Genesis says that when God created man, he created him out of clay and breath. Clay is visible; breath is invisible. Through poetic language, the author of Genesis is sharing with us a very foundational truth about human beings—we are both body and soul, not one or the other, but both/and. Human beings are not just spirits as Plato or Descartes believed, and we're not just bodies as so many believe today. As human beings, we are both body and soul.

In addition to being both body and soul, God also created us male and female. John Paul II wrote an entire work basically unpacking that truth in his *Theology of the Body.* Christopher West, a popular commentator on Theology of the Body, likes to say that a man's body makes absolutely no sense without a woman's body, and that a woman's body makes absolutely no sense without a man's body. He's right.

That humanity is composed of both men and women may seem rather obvious, but Catholicism has always highlighted this distinction and is very cautious about any of culture's attempts to blur it. Both men and women are created in God's image and likeness, and men and women are both equal in dignity, yet men and women remain different. Our bodies are different, and that difference is important. In fact, that difference is one of the most privileged ways we have to understand what kind of relationship God wants to have with his people.

God wants to be close to us, to be one with us, in union, in communion, in harmony, in rhythm, and for all time. What is the best way for human beings to understand what that union might look like? It looks like marriage—specifically, the marital act. A man and woman who enter into the covenant of marriage have a love that is always incarnate, always embodied, for as human beings we can't love without our bodies. (This isn't to say that all love is sexual, for most love is not, but all love is embodied, because we are bodily beings.) A man's body is made to enter a woman, and a woman's body is designed to receive a man, so that a man and woman can literally become one body. This has the potential to create new life, which is the bodily manifestation of the kind of relationship that God wants to have with us.

The Catholic Church takes a lot of heat for her teachings in the arena of human sexuality, but most of the criticism comes from people who misunderstand what the Church actually teaches. For Catholics, sex is for marriage, because marriage is the embodied sign of Christ's union with his Church. Jesus is the Bridegroom and we, the Church, are his Bride, and he came to be one with us. That life-giving *one-ness* is embodied by a man and a woman in the sacrament of Marriage. So to truly understand the Church's teaching on sexuality, one must always keep in mind that God made us in his image and likeness and therefore created sex with specific meaning.

The both/and principle comes into play in the sexual realm in that Catholics believe that genital expression is only proper in the context of marriage, and that each and every act of sex must be both procreative and unitive, because that's the kind of love that God has for us—a love that is procreative and unitive. This doesn't mean that every time a husband and wife come together in the marital embrace they are trying to have a baby, but it does mean that they don't bring any unnatural thing into the marital act that would prevent life from being conceived. It also means that human life is meant to be conceived within the marital act. Children themselves have that right. It's also worth noting that because children come to be through the union of a man and a woman, only a man can be a father and only a woman can be a mother. (This reality of fatherhood and motherhood is foundational to understanding the "fatherhood" of male priesthood as well. That is, if only a man can be a father, and a priest is a father, then only a man can be a priest. In addition, the priest stands in the place of Christ, the Bridegroom of the Church. This can only be properly represented by a male figure.[*])

---

[*] For more on this important topic, see *The Catholic Priesthood and Women: A Guide to the Teaching of the Church* by Sara Butler (Chicago: Hillenbrand books, 2007). —*Ed.*

The Life of the Church

Is the Church the hierarchical institution founded by Christ (who gave the keys of the kingdom to Peter), or is the Church the People of God? It's both. I find it funny that when Catholics complain about the Church and say that the Church needs to change, they are almost always speaking of Church in the first sense. But when they are speaking about the Church in the second sense, it's as if the Church is a spotless bride. The fact is that the Church is both the institution and the People of God. The Church is also the Bride of Christ, a community of disciples, a mission, a hospital for sinners, a shelter from the storm, and a living sacrament.

Is the Church progressive or traditional? Again, it's both. At the Second Vatican Council, two very important movements were at hand: *aggiornamento* and *ressourcement*. Depending on where you study your theology, professors will argue that one or the other was really at the heart of Vatican II, but the truth is that they worked together and were most complementary. *Aggiornamento* is an Italian word that means "bringing up to date." In many ways, the Second Vatican Council was about figuring out how the Church can be her best self in the modern world. *Ressourcement* is a French word that basically means "renewal by returning to the sources." Which sources? The Church Fathers and Doctors, especially Thomas Aquinas *as* Thomas Aquinas and not a dry, neo-scholastic version of him. So at the Second Vatican Council, the council fathers were both looking back and looking forward in order to be rooted in the Tradition, and to appropriate that Tradition so that it would flourish.

Is the Catholic Church a Church of Scripture or a Church of Tradition? It's both. The earliest books of the New Testament were not even written until AD 50. But Pentecost happened twenty years before that. So the Church was already established and growing before what we now know as the New Testament ever existed. Jesus entrusted his Church to Peter and the Apostles, and he sent the Holy Spirit upon them to guide them. That same Spirit worked through those apostolic successors when compiling the books that make up what we know as the Bible. Scripture and Tradition work together, they inform each other, and neither makes sense without the other.

Is the Catholic Church a Church of faith or works? Catholics believe that salvation comes through Jesus Christ, who suffered and died to take away the sins of the world. It is through him, and only through him, that we can find our salvation. But it is also true that a relationship with Jesus and accepting the gift of salvation that he offers us should make us become like him. Our faith should manifest itself in our works. The life of faith that we live should incarnate our relationship with God, as we feed the hungry, give drink to the thirsty, clothe the naked, shelter the homeless, visit the sick and imprisoned, and bury the dead. Good works themselves do not bring about salvation, but neither does faith without action. Both faith and works together capture real Catholic living.

Is the Catholic Church a community of saints or sinners? It's both. As a matter of fact, with the exception of Our Lady, every saint was once a sinner. I once heard Matt Maher say that the reason God makes us first admit we are a sinner in order to become a saint is so that we wouldn't take all the credit. It's true. We can appreciate grace only as sinners. In his first interview as pope, Pope Francis was asked, "Who is Jorge Bergoglio?" He responded, "I am a sinner whom the Lord has looked upon." That is the perfect formulation of Christian spirituality. Like someone in a twelve-step program, the first step to recovery is admitting that you have a problem. The universal problem of humanity is that we're all born with original sin, and the only way to heal from it is to first admit that we have a problem. Then, of course, we go to the One who can heal us from our illness, the One who is our remedy, the One who can make us saints. In our weakness, we find our strength.

Is the Church about the clergy or the laity? It's about both, and at the same time. The clergy exist to serve the laity, and the laity count on the clergy to bring them the Sacraments as well as to teach, preach, and govern. The laity are called to be salt, light, and leaven in the world, to bring Christ to the parts of the world that only they can. A great description of the kind of relationship that clergy and laity ought to have is found in the First Eucharist Prayer for Various Needs: "Strengthen the bond of unity between the faithful and the pastors of your people, together with (*N.*), our Pope, (*N.*), our Bishop, and the whole Order of Bishops, that in a world torn by strife your people may shine forth as a prophetic sign of unity and concord." As Saint Paul says, the Church is a body, and we are all different parts (see 1 Cor 12:12–27). The Church flourishes when we all play our parts well and let each part do what it is supposed to do— and that goes for clergy and laity alike.

Are we a Church of Good Friday and suffering or a Church of Easter Sunday and joy? In Catholicism it's always both. We would never even celebrate Good Friday if Jesus did not rise from the dead on Easter Sunday. But unless Jesus died on Good Friday, his resurrection on Easter Sunday would have no meaning. Christian living is about dying and rising, each and every day, especially on the last day. If you try to save your life, you will lose it, but if you lose your life, you will save it. Unless a grain of wheat falls to the ground and dies, it will not have life within in it, but if it dies, it will have life abundantly (see Jn 12:24–25). This dying and rising is the Paschal Mystery, which is at the heart of all things Catholic. Trying to ignore either dying or rising will leave you quite lopsided.

Are Catholics a people of faith or a people of reason? As already mentioned, a great lie of modernity is that one has to choose between faith and reason, as if the two contradict each other. They don't. God has endowed each and every human being with an intellect by which we can come to know the world. Science, especially modern science, is the friend of Catholicism. (Recall who first posited the Big Bang theory.) Faith does not compete with reason or science. Faith actually broadens reason so that we can know more about reality, with the help of God's revelation, than we could ever come to know on our own.

How about the Mass? Is the both/and principle present there? Yes. It's all over the place. Churches are made of stone and glass, marble and wood. The assembly consists of clergy and laity. There is the Liturgy of the Word and the Liturgy of the Eucharist. We read from the Old Testament and New Testament, from the Gospels and the Epistles. We sit and we stand, we bow and we genuflect, we kneel and we stand again. The altar is a table, and the table is an altar. The Eucharist is both a meal and a sacrifice. The Eucharist is the Body of Christ and the community gathered is also the Body of Christ. The Eucharist is both the Body and the Blood of Christ. The homily should be both challenging and comforting, the music should be sacred yet singable, and we participate both in song and in silence. The Mass is happening here and now, but it's also a participation in the eternal wedding feast in heaven. The Mass prepares us to bring Christ to the world, but it calls us back to be fed each and every week. The Mass is for my salvation and the salvation of the world. The Mass puts the Catholic both/and principle on full display. It is the source and summit of the Christian life.

Politics

Surely the Catholic Church cannot maintain her both/and position when it comes to politics, can she? Indeed she can, and she does. Perhaps the best example of this principle in recent years was on display during Pope Francis' visit to the United States in September 2015. The United States of America can be a very divided country where far too often Democrats and Republicans refuse to speak to each other, let alone work together for the betterment of the country. On the third day of Pope Francis' visit, he made history by being the first pope to address a joint session of Congress, and one of his major points was to encourage encounter and dialogue within Congress.

Throughout his visit to the United States, Pope Francis was brilliant in the way he went about addressing all important issues as *human* (and therefore Catholic) *issues*: the poor, the unborn, the elderly, religious liberty, the environment, marriage, family, immigration, and the economy. Such issues normally divide our country by political affiliation, but Pope Francis was working to encourage us all to see the both/and perspective of Catholicism on life and all of creation. It was a challenge for all Americans to broaden their vision in order to accept a fuller view of the created world.

Pope Francis was also brilliant in his both/and gestures, meeting with the president, dignitaries, and wealthy donors, while also making plenty of time to be with prisoners, the disabled, and the poor. God's celebrities. He also spoke and prayed in English, Spanish, and Latin. Yet perhaps the most both/and, Catholic/political thing Pope Francis did during his visit to the United States was the speech he gave at Independence Hall in Philadelphia on both religious liberty and immigration—in the same address! Sometimes religious liberty is considered a Republican issue and immigration is considered a Democratic issue, but the reality is more complex. Religious liberty is a fundamental right, and people can have varying views on immigration policy. Pope Francis was able to show that both are human issues and that one can support religious liberty and immigration. The Holy Father made many people uncomfortable that afternoon, from both sides of the aisle. But that's good, because Catholics need to be Catholic before they are even American, let alone Democrat or Republican. The Church rises above American politics and includes what we as Americans often see only in terms of a political party. The full truth is that Pope Francis also comforted many people that afternoon because Catholicism, at its best, both cuts and heals, often at the same time.

The Ultimate Both/And Reality

It shouldn't be surprising that the both/and principle, according to its very own principle, can't stand on its own. That is, in order for the both/and to work, it needs to be partnered with another principle: the either/or. Although I haven't explicitly treated this principle until now, this book wouldn't make sense without it. God exists or God doesn't exist. Jesus is true God or Jesus isn't true God. Jesus is true man or Jesus isn't true man. Mary is the Mother of God or Mary isn't the Mother of God.

Jesus rose from the dead or Jesus didn't rise from the dead. Jesus founded the Church upon the rock of Peter or Jesus didn't found the Church upon the rock of Peter. In philosophy we call this either/or principle the principle of non-contradiction, or the *PNC*, and it is the foundation for all both/and realities listed above. I find this pairing of the either/or and the both/and to be the most intellectually satisfying both/and example of Catholicism.

By the time I entered college seminary in the fall of 1994, Guns N' Roses was out and grunge rock was in. Bands like Nirvana, Pearl Jam, Soundgarden, Stone Temple Pilots, Alice in Chains, and Rage Against the Machine replaced the hair metal bands of the 80s, and I very much liked the new sound. As a seminarian and a philosophy major, I started to spend a lot more time researching the bands I listened to and reading the biographies of my favorite artists. I paid special attention to their family histories, and was especially interested in their religious upbringing, if there was one.

As a seminarian, I no longer wanted to be a rock star, but I did learn to sing and to play the guitar and harmonica. A few of us seminarians formed a little band and played a lot of the music of the day, but we also wrote some of our own music, which was edifying. I was the worst musician in the band, but I was still in a band. I was learning a lot about teamwork, hard work, discipline, and creativity. I had learned all that in one way through athletics when I was younger, but now as a young adult playing music, it was coming at me at a deeper level.

A few years later, I was ordained a priest and was assigned to Saint Mary Parish in Hudson, Ohio. The parish held a big fundraiser every year to support its youth ministry. To help support the teens, the parochial vicar would auction off some of his talent in the live auction. Priests who had been there before me had gifts in the culinary arts and deep appreciation for American history, so they offered to cook a meal for twelve or to be a guide on a historic walking tour through downtown Hudson. I didn't have those gifts, but I could play some guitar and I knew a few songs, so I auctioned myself to play a concert at a parishioner's house. It was a big hit, and word got around. The next year I put a little band together with the music minister and some of the talented teen musicians from the parish. We raised a lot of money over the years for the parish's LifeTeen ministry, for vocation support, and for mission trips.

We still get together a couple times a year to play a fundraiser, and we play a lot of the music that I loved as a kid and as a young adult: Springsteen, Guns N' Roses, and Pearl Jam. Sometimes I'll change some inappropriate lyrics, but for the most part, we pick songs that get people dancing, singing along, and having a good Catholic time.

At the very end of Mark's Gospel, Jesus tells his disciples they will be able to handle serpents and drink poison and not be harmed. I understand those words to mean that the serpents and the poison are the culture. If you are not grounded in the Gospel, you'll be killed by such things, but if you are grounded in the Gospel, you will be able to handle those things and not be harmed by them. That's the Catholic both/and principle at work.

Certainly some things are either/or, but when it comes to me being a priest and enjoying secular music, that's a both/and.

8

Loving the Bomb

An Answer to Suffering

"And you yourself a sword will pierce."

— *Luke 2:35*

"What people don't realize is how much religion costs. They think faith is a big electric blanket, when of course it is the cross."

— *Flannery O'Connor*

WHEN YOU ARE YOUNG, your parents take care of you. When your parents get old, you help take care of your parents. Many families have a good twenty, thirty, or even forty years between those two moments, when both parents and their adult children are healthy and can carry on what I would call an "adult friendship," a friendship in which neither child nor parent needs caregiving. No matter how long it lasts, this time is a blessed time indeed.

I was a sophomore in college seminary when I realized that my relationship with my parents had changed to the *adult friendship* status. Of course, I was still their son, and they were still my mom and dad, but our relationship took on a new dynamic. They no longer needed to discipline me (as the seminary was doing that important work for me, and I started doing a lot of that work for myself). Our conversations became more natural and substantive, and I really began to appreciate all the heroic sacrifices that my parents had made to raise me, feed me, house me, educate me, and literally show me what the Catholic faith looked like by their own lives.

But in 2000 my dad became legally blind. He was working a side job when he felt a pop in his right eye and the center of his vision immediately went black. My dad had lost the vision in his left eye from macular degeneration back in 1986, and normally the vision of the other eye goes within six months to a year. To make it fourteen years without losing the vision in his right eye was a minor miracle. With one good eye, my dad was able to see me graduate from high school and, four years later, watch me receive my college diploma. But he would never be able to clearly see my face, or anyone's face, again.

The best way to understand my dad's vision is to hold two fists up in front of your eyes so that you can't see anything straight ahead, only the periphery. He also suffered from glaucoma, so the macular degeneration made his already bad vision even worse. He had to sit about one foot away from the TV screen to see anything. Needless to say, life changed for him.

My mom worked quickly to make their home friendly to his low vision, using a variety of colored bubble pens to mark knobs, buttons, and dials on the stove, microwave, washer, and dryer, so that he could feel what he was doing around the house. We also bought him a TV remote with big buttons and a phone with even bigger buttons, including preset buttons for one-push calls. But as much as we tried to make things easier for him, he had lost his ability to read, to drive, and to see faces, and all those losses weighed on him.

To make things even harder, it was right around this time that my mom was diagnosed with liver cancer. By the grace of God and with the help of chemotherapy she had already beat cancer three times, so my dad and my brother and I encouraged her to try the chemo route again. Since my dad could no longer drive, I took her to her chemo appointments. After a few months of some serious treatments, her doctor told us that the spots on her liver were growing bigger and that the chemo wasn't working. My mom decided that she was too tired to fight anymore and that she had had it with chemotherapy and all its side effects.

So my dad was blind and my mom was dying of cancer. And because my dad couldn't see much of anything, he had a hard time caring for my mom at home. He couldn't read her prescription bottles or see the little pills she had to take for pain management. After only five years of *friendship status* with my parents, Adam and I became their caregivers. Visits to Mom and Dad's house were no longer for rest and meals; they were for shopping, appointments, running errands, and cutting the lawn.

Could it get any worse for the Ference family? Yes! Just then, my brother, who was engaged to be married, received the surprise of his life when his fiancée unexpectedly called off the wedding. He was crushed.

Everybody in my family was hurting. And because they were all hurting, I was hurting too. Why did all these bad things happen? And why did they all happen at once? Why do bad things happen to good people? What does it all mean? And if God is all good, why does he allow his people to suffer? Where is God in all of this mess? Where is God in the midst of our suffering?

The Origin of Suffering

This final chapter deals with the question of suffering—the perennial question. In every generation people suffer, and in every generation people wonder what to make of suffering. If you are reading this book, chances are that you have suffered, and likely you have suffered much more than I have. So what do we make of suffering? And what role does it play in the life of faith? Moreover, what role does God play in our experience of suffering?

To begin with, let's remember the stories of our origin and the origin of the created world presented in the first two chapters of Genesis. God created the world and all things in it not because he was lonely and needed friends, but because as a community of persons in the Trinity, the Triune God wanted to share himself. He wanted to give himself away. He wanted to pour out his love generously. The first chapter of Genesis tells us that everything God created is good, and that human beings, made in his image and likeness, are the pinnacle of his creation. The second chapter of Genesis tells the story of all of creation, and then of the marriage between the first man and the first woman, which analogically displays the marriage between God and his people. But when the man and the woman chose to sin rather than to love, when they began to see God as their competitor rather than their Creator, things changed drastically. Before the Fall, everything was in proper order and our relationship with God, with each other, and with all of his creation was in perfect harmony. After the Fall, our relationship with God—and even our relationship with creation—changed. Suffering and death became a reality, and Eden was no longer our home. That's how Genesis tells the story.

For our purposes, it is important that we glean a few important theological points from Genesis. The first point is that everything God created is good, because God is good and all creation comes from God. The second point is that before the Fall there was no sin, sorrow, suffering, or death. The third point is that it was our first parents, and not God, who brought sin into the world by choosing to do their own will rather than the will of God. In other words, human beings—not God—are responsible for the break in the relationship between humanity and God that we call the Fall. Fourth, the Fall ruptured not only our relationship with God but also our relationship with creation. Human beings and the world remained good, but their fallen state needed redemption. Fifth, there was no way that we could save ourselves from the Fall; we needed (and still need) a Savior.

Since the Fall, human beings have experienced suffering, which manifests itself in many ways—most obvious is the fact that everybody dies. No one can escape death, no matter how hard you might try. What pain and sadness people have endured over the loss of a loved one! Death has many causes. Some are natural, like a flood, a hurricane, or a volcano. Other causes of death originate in someone's deliberate plan to fly a plane into a building, shoot up a school, drive into a crowd of people, or take one's own life. Others are accidental, as in the case of an overdose, a car accident, a fall, or a drowning. Sometimes we even say that people died of "natural causes," meaning that they didn't die in any of the ways above, but that they died of cancer, heart failure, or in their sleep.

But other significant experiences of suffering besides death are worth noting. Although sickness, disease, and injury may not lead to death, they surely can cause suffering and make life difficult. We also experience heartbreak when relationships rupture. How much pain is caused by family feuds, fights between friends, fallouts between siblings, separation, and divorce! Such breaks in relationship have many causes, including miscommunication, infidelity, betrayal, dishonesty, duplicity, immaturity, irresponsibility, and the inability to keep a promise. (I'm sure that if I left a couple of blank pages at the end of this book entitled "experiences and causes of suffering," you could easily fill those pages with many more examples.) The point is that since the Fall, suffering has become an inescapable part of human existence. The question is, what is the Catholic response to the problem of suffering?

Suffering in the Holy Family

Like all the important questions about Catholicism, the answer is wrapped up and revealed in the incarnation. The Second Person of the Trinity became one of us in the person of Jesus Christ so that we could become like him, or, even more precisely, so that we could become him. We've already treated the bizarre reality that Jesus Christ was not born in a pristine palace, a fancy mansion, or a sterile hospital room. On the contrary, the King of the Universe was born in a messy stable in Bethlehem. Now let's take a closer look at the situations of his mother, Mary, and his stepfather, Joseph, and the details of Jesus' birth. Those details offer important information regarding the question of suffering and will prepare us for the ultimate response to human suffering found in the incarnation.

In Luke's Gospel, when the Angel Gabriel appears to Mary and greets her with "Hail, favored one! The Lord is with you," Mary does not respond with delight. On the contrary, Luke tells us, "She was greatly troubled at what was said and pondered what sort of greeting this might be" (1:28–29). To be deeply troubled is serious business, and that's where Mary found herself. We could say that she was surprised, shocked, or even scared by Gabriel's presence and greeting. We know that she eventually consents to being the Mother of Jesus with her great *fiat*, but it wasn't easy for her.

We know from Scripture that Mary conceived the Second Person of the Trinity within her womb by the power of the Holy Spirit, but would others in her own community of Nazareth believe such an explanation? Would she even tell anyone besides Joseph about Gabriel's visit? It's likely that most of the people in her community believed she was pregnant with Joseph's child. Imagine all the thoughts that must have been going through Mary's head, and how she repeatedly returned to her conversation with Gabriel in her memory, trying to make sense of her situation.

When it came time to give birth, Mary and Joseph had to travel all the way to Bethlehem for the census. Because they couldn't find any lodging, they wound up in a stable with the animals. According to Scripture, this was where Mary gave birth to Jesus. After a long journey, a young, first-time mother gave birth in a stable to a son she conceived without sexual relations and layed him in a manger, without her mother, midwife, or friends. But there's more. An angel told some shepherds that the Savior had been born, and they made their way to the manger to see her newborn child. Think about that: a new mom who just gave birth for the very first time is visited in the middle of the night by shepherds—complete strangers—and they want to see her baby. What could she do? What did she do? Luke tells us, "Mary kept all these things, reflecting on them in her heart" (Lk 2:19). Mary knew that what she was going through was challenging, tiring, painful, and even bizarre, yet she trusted that God would provide for her and that God would keep his promise to her. A few weeks later, she was told by Simeon that, on account of her newborn son, her heart would be pierced with a sword (see Lk 2:35). As she did with Gabriel's message, Mary must have played Simeon's words over and over again in her mind and heart, trying to make sense of their meaning.

Why spend so much time on Mary in this chapter on suffering? Because before we look to the incarnation himself, it serves us well to study the situation of the Mother of the incarnate Christ. Mary's life was not easy; she knew suffering, pain, struggle, and hardship. Being the Mother of God did not spare Mary from having her heart pierced on account of her child. But Mary did not run from suffering or try to numb herself or curse God for making her suffer. Her response? "His mother kept all these things in her heart" (Lk 2:51). In other words, she sat with the suffering and trusted that God would make good of it.

Mary's husband, Joseph, also dealt with his share of suffering. His wife became pregnant without him ever having sexual relations with her. We don't know whether he initially thought Mary became pregnant through an act of adultery or if he thought that being the stepfather of the Son of God was beyond him. But we do know that, because he was a just man, Joseph planned to divorce Mary quietly to save her from ridicule. But in a dream, an angel of the Lord appeared to him and said, "Joseph, son of David, do not be afraid to take Mary your wife into your home. For it is through the holy Spirit that this child has been conceived in her" (Mt 1:20). So Joseph does as the angel directed, takes Mary into his home, and eventually travels with her to Bethlehem. But Matthew's Gospel tells us that after Jesus' birth and after the visit of the Magi, Joseph had another dream warning him of Herod's planned massacre of all the infant boys of Bethlehem, so Joseph took Mary and Jesus and traveled with them to Egypt for safety.

We look to the life of Joseph for the same reason we look to the life of Mary, because the stepfather of the incarnation shows us something about suffering. No one escapes suffering. Joseph responded to suffering in the same way that Mary did: by entering into it with faith, trusting that God would somehow make good of a bad situation.

The Suffering Servant

We've seen thus far that suffering is a part of the human experience, even for the Holy Family. Mary and Joseph both had their own experiences of real suffering to which they responded in faith, trusting that God would somehow bring good out of the bad. It's now time to turn toward the Incarnation himself and see how God responds to the question of suffering in the person of Jesus Christ. What can the Son of God teach us about the experience and meaning of our suffering?

Remember that in Jesus Christ, who is true God and true man, God becomes one of us—like us in all things but sin. This means that in the incarnation, the Son of God experiences everything that we experience as human beings, including our experience of the fallen world, and specifically our experience of suffering.

It would be easy to jump right into the passion narratives of the Gospels and show how Jesus suffered a terrible passion and death as evidence that he knew the reality of suffering, and we will certainly get to those narratives in time. But in many ways, the entire life of Jesus was a life of suffering, just as the life of every human being is a life of suffering. Consider your own life for a moment. Has there ever been a year, or a month, or a week when you were completely free from some experience of suffering? It's not likely. So it makes sense that the life of the Incarnation would also be a life filled with suffering.

The first experience of Christ's suffering was likely at his circumcision, eight days after his birth. I have never seen a circumcision performed, and I don't remember my own, but I am certain that being circumcised is not a pleasant experience. It involves significant suffering for both the infant boy and his parents. (At his circumcision, the Incarnation bleeds for the first time and he receives the name Jesus, which means "God saves." This prefigures that Jesus will eventually save us through his own blood.) The Gospels offer even more accounts of Jesus' suffering. He was often tired, or hungry, or thirsty. He suffered when his Apostles failed to understand his teachings and when the citizens of his hometown rejected him. Jesus wept at the death of his good friend Lazarus as well as over the city of Jerusalem. Although the Gospels don't offer an account of Joseph's death, Jesus would certainly have experienced suffering as he grieved the death of his virtuous stepfather.

We shouldn't be surprised that Jesus comes to us as one who suffers. Centuries before God ever became one of us in the person of Jesus Christ, the Old Testament Prophet Isaiah dedicated an entire chapter to the way in which God would save his people by becoming the *Suffering Servant*. At the Good Friday liturgy, Catholics read Chapter 53 of Isaiah, which offers a detailed account and foreshadows Christ's passion:

> He was spurned and avoided by men,
>> a man of suffering, knowing pain,
> Like one from whom you turn your face,
>> spurned, and we held him in no esteem.
>
> Yet it was our pain that he bore,
>> our sufferings he endured.
> We thought of him as stricken,
>> struck down by God and afflicted,
> But he was pierced for our sins,
>> crushed for our iniquity.
> He bore the punishment that makes us whole,
>> by his wounds we were healed. (Is 53:3–5)

It's haunting how accurately Isaiah descriptively predicts Christ's eventual passion and death. Without going through each passion narrative to show how Isaiah's vision is fulfilled in the Gospel accounts, we can note the most salient aspects of Christ's passion.

As Jesus gathered his Apostles around him at the Last Supper, he knew that he was going to be delivered to death. He also knew that one of those handpicked Apostles would betray him. That night when Judas betrayed him, Jesus asked the rest of his Apostles to stay with him and pray. What happened? They all fell asleep, leaving Jesus alone and sweating blood just when he most needed their friendship. Moreover, Peter, whose name means "the Rock," crumbled under pressure. When questioned about his friendship with Jesus, Peter denied that he even knew him not once, but three times. Then Jesus was arrested and ridiculed before the Sanhedrin and, although innocent, suffered a terrible scourging under Pontius Pilate. (If you can handle it, view Mel Gibson's *The Passion of the Christ* to get a sense of what this practice entailed.) Amid the jeering of the crowds, Jesus was led away, carrying a cross to Calvary where he would be crucified, wearing a crown of thorns around his head. The journey to Golgotha was brutal, and so was the treatment he received not only from the soldiers but also from the crowds. Once he arrived at Golgotha, he was stripped of his garments, which was yet another form of humiliation, and crucified between two criminals. We know of seven sayings that Jesus spoke from the pulpit of his cross, but for our purposes I want to focus on two of them, the first from the Gospel of Mark and the second from the Gospel of Luke.

First, Jesus cried out, "My God, my God, why have you forsaken me?" (Mt 27:46). At first glance it may seem as if Jesus has lost all hope in God, the Father. But upon a closer look, we see that Jesus is actually praying the first line of Psalm 22, which is perhaps the most important psalm of the entire Psalter. Like Isaiah 53, Psalm 22 is an Old Testament reference to the Messiah and predicts that the Savior will go through terrible suffering and unspeakable torment in order to bring about his saving work. As the psalm progresses, we realize that this psalm is not ultimately about despair, but that it names the undeniable reality of suffering as the way to bring about redemption. Although the psalm may commence with a tone of despair, by verse 25 the psalmist announces, "For he has not spurned or disdained the misery of this poor wretch, / Did not turn away from me, but heard me when I cried out." (The Father has not abandoned the Son. He has heard his Son's cry.) Jesus never denies his experience of suffering, nor does he deny the Father's love for him. But with a wholehearted cry to the Father from the deepest part of his being, Jesus, the Son of God incarnates Psalm 22 in his bloody, torn, and suffering person.

In the Gospel of Luke, we are told that just before Jesus died, he uttered another loud cry: "Father, into your hands I commend my spirit" (23:46). Again, we see that in the midst of the worst suffering imaginable, with his final breath, Jesus hands over everything that he is—including his suffering and pain—to his Father. In a strange way, Jesus makes himself a gift to the Father, and his suffering is an important part of that gift. The mystery of our salvation unfolds in the gift of Jesus' passion and death. There we find our salvation, but it doesn't happen immediately.

Jesus would have to be taken down from the cross and buried before he could rise from the dead in his glorified body. Yet recall how people recognized him when he did rise from the dead on the third day—by his wounds, which are a sign of the Suffering Servant. Even the two disciples on the road to Emmaus recognized him in the breaking of the bread, which was no ordinary bread but the Eucharist—Christ's Body, broken for us.

The Meaning of Suffering

So what does this all mean? We see now that no one can escape the reality of human suffering, not Mary, not Joseph, and especially not Jesus Christ himself. On the contrary, the Son of God goes through some of the worst suffering documented in human history. But even though he rose from the dead three days later, and is now seated at the right hand of the Father, two thousand years later we still suffer. Jesus may have taken away the sins of the world through the gift of himself on the cross of Calvary, but why didn't he take away human suffering once and for all?

In a sense, he did. When Jesus gave his life away on the cross and three days later rose from the dead, he beat death itself and opened for us the way to the Father for all eternity. But for us, the only way to inherit that life of eternity is by following him, which means following him through death. At Baptism, we die to sin and are born into the life of grace, but to fully enter into eternal life, we first need to pass through death. Until we actually pass through death ourselves, we have a lifetime of opportunity to practice dying through human suffering.

Jesus did not take away our earthly suffering when he died on the cross, but he did enter into it with all its ugliness and pain and he gave it meaning. He showed by his own life, death, and resurrection that God, the Father, can bring good out of bad. Although we may not see that good right away, or perhaps never see it on this side of the veil, the Father keeps his promises. Death never has the final say. Neither does suffering.

The meaning of suffering is ultimately a mystery, but in Christianity, the Paschal Mystery—the dying and rising of Jesus—gives meaning to suffering. It matters that the Son of God came to earth and knew suffering firsthand all the days of his life. It matters that our God is not far from our human experience but entered into it with his entire being, even to the point of his terrible passion and death. It is comforting to gaze upon a crucifix or an image of the *Pietà* and reflect upon our God's willingness to be one with us, not just in our joys but also in our sufferings. Christ's willingness to enter into our suffering puts God's self-emptying, mysterious, sacrificial love on full display.

At Christmastime, Christians love to sing songs about the birth of Jesus, and rightly so. In the incarnation, God became one of us and we call him Emmanuel, "God with us." But the title *Emmanuel* is just as important at the end of Jesus' life as it is at the beginning. We may suffer, but we are never alone in our suffering. God is with us.

I want to tell you about a Catholic man and the suffering he endured. He's not a priest, but he does teach PSR (Parish School of Religion) at his home parish in New York City, and he happens to be the host of his own late night talk show on CBS. His name is Stephen Colbert. When he was only ten years old, his father and his two brothers closest to him in age died in a plane crash.

Colbert claims that when he joined the world-famous *Second City* in Chicago, he received the most important lesson of his life. The first night of his professional debut, the stage director told him, "You have to learn to love the bomb." Colbert said, "It took me a long time to really understand what that meant. It wasn't 'Don't worry, you'll get it next time.' It wasn't 'Laugh it off.' No, it means what it says. You gotta learn to *love* when you're failing. . . . The embracing of that, the discomfort of failing in front of an audience, leads you to penetrate through the fear that blinds you."[1]

We live in a culture that teaches us that we must do whatever it takes to avoid suffering. Have a drink, pop a pill, sleep around, stay super busy, work harder, stare at a screen, or do whatever you need to do in order to avoid the reality of suffering. Yet the Lord himself entered into the reality of human experience, going through everything that we go through, including suffering and death. He even predicted to his disciples that he would have to be rejected, suffer, and be put to death before he would be raised on the third day. Peter tried to tell Jesus that he wouldn't have to endure such terrible things, and to that Jesus said, "Get behind me, Satan." In other words, Christ's mission to save us from sin does not avoid suffering and death but actually depends upon it. Jesus didn't promise to take away our suffering here on earth, but he did come to give meaning to our suffering—to show us that suffering is not in vain, and that suffering can actually be sacred.

When Colbert was asked how in the world he could be so grounded and joyful after having lost his dad and brothers at such a young age, he responded, "MY MOTHER . . . the answer is: my mother." He explained, "I was raised in a Catholic tradition. I'll start there. That's my context for my existence, that I am here to know God, love God, serve God, that we might be happy with each other in this world and with Him in the next—the catechism. That makes a lot of sense to me. I got that from my mom. And my dad. And my siblings." Colbert continued, "I was left alone a lot after Dad and the boys died. . . . And it was just me and Mom for a long time. And by her example I am not bitter. By *her* example. She was not. Broken, yes. Bitter, no." Colbert then insisted that "to recognize that our sorrow is inseparable from our joy is always to understand suffering, ourselves, in the light of eternity."[2]

Stephen Colbert is a witness to the faithful acceptance of suffering, which he learned from his Catholic mother. But he's careful to point out that acceptance of suffering "does not mean being defeated by suffering." He explains, "You gotta learn to love the bomb. Boy, did I have a bomb when I was 10. That was quite an explosion. And I learned to love it. So that's why. Maybe, I don't know. That might be why you don't see me as someone angry and working out my demons onstage. It's that I love the thing that I most wish had not happened."[3]

If you are reading this book, chances are that you have suffered. And maybe your suffering was terrible. And maybe you are suffering right now. Suffering is part of the human experience, and if you live long enough, you can't avoid it. This is why Jesus enters into the very heart of suffering and calls Peter "Satan" when he tries to insist that Jesus avoid suffering. If Jesus, who is God, is like us in all things but sin, those things include suffering and death. God may not take away our suffering in this world, but through Jesus he does give meaning to our suffering, and he shows us that we are not alone in our suffering, and that our suffering is not in vain.

As you know by now, after a long struggle with cancer, my mom went home to the Lord a little over a year before I was ordained a priest. That was a pretty difficult time in my life. I'll spare you all the details, but trust me when I tell you that I suffered, and I wondered what God was doing. Fourteen years later, I have some clarity in the matter, and I have experienced the resurrection in a very tangible way. Because I spent so much time with my mom as she was dying of cancer, and because I was at her bedside when she took her last breath, I can attest that since then I have never been afraid of hospitals, nursing homes, emergency rooms, hospices, dying people, dead people, or anything like that. That may sound strange, but it's a wonderful thing for a priest. My mom taught me how to love life and even love death, which is the way to eternal life for those who believe.

My mother taught me how to *learn to love the bomb*, which is basically Colbert's way of saying to learn to love the cross, or to learn to love suffering. Colbert doesn't say that we need to love suffering in some masochistic way, but to love it because suffering is a mysterious gift from God. He quotes Tolkien who writes, "What punishments of God are not gifts?" and then explains, "So it would be ungrateful not to take *everything* with gratitude. It doesn't mean you want it. I can hold both of those ideas in my head. . . . Oh, I'm grateful. Oh, I feel terrible."[4]

I get that. When I think about my mom's death, my dad's blindness, and my brother's broken engagement, I wish that those things had never happened the way they did, and I hate them. But at the very same time, I am grateful that they happened exactly the way they did, and I love them. That's the mystery of suffering, and the power of the Paschal Mystery.

Epilogue

Fiat

"May it be done to me
according to your word."

— *Luke 1:38*

"It is Mary's obedience that
opens the door to God."

— *Pope Benedict XVI*

"Lord keep me. Mother help
me."

— *Flannery O'Connor*

BY BEGINNING EACH CHAPTER of this book with a personal
narrative, I attempted to show what Catholicism looks like in real
life. Since Catholicism is incarnational by its very nature, the last
thing that I wanted to do was to write in abstractions. After the
belief that God became man in the person of Jesus Christ, one
of the most incarnational beliefs of Catholicism is that God has a
Mother. My goal for this final section is not to offer a theological

treatise on the *Theotokos*, but rather to do what Catholics tend to do, that is, to honor Our Lady at the end of a work.

Take a look at any recent papal letter and you'll see that popes always conclude their writing by honoring the Blessed Virgin Mary. (Remember that the Fourth Commandment is "Honor your father and mother," and Jesus had a mother. If we are to imitate Jesus in all things, then honoring his mother must be one of them.) In convents, monasteries, and seminaries around the world, Catholic communities end each day by singing a Marian hymn after praying Compline. Mary is a big deal because the Second Person of the Trinity was conceived within her. Mary literally delivered Jesus to the world and became the perfect disciple of Jesus.

When I entered the college seminary, I had a pretty strong Marian devotion, and it grew with each year of my priestly formation. I meditated on Mary in the Scriptures, I prayed the Rosary regularly, and I even sketched a bunch of pictures of Mary in my prayer journal. But about a year before I was ordained, most of that stopped. I didn't realize it at the time, and it wasn't until about five years into priesthood that anyone pointed out to me that I had neglected the Mother of God.

One of the young women from my youth group at Saint Mary's Parish, my first assignment, wrote me when I was studying at CUA. Alison was in her senior year of college. In her letter, she lovingly expressed gratitude for the important role that I had played as her priest in her life of faith, which was a welcome affirmation. But she also told me that she hoped I would grow closer to Our Lady, and she enclosed a rosary that she had made with her own hands. I was honored by her gift and challenged by her invitation. I realized that she was right about my relationship with the Mother of Jesus: it was lacking.

At Alison's invitation, I began to pray with my new gift daily. I had to memorize the Luminous Mysteries, but other than that, it was fairly easy to get back into the habit of praying the Rosary. I prayed it when I walked, and I walked almost every day. There's a beautiful, calming rhythm about the Rosary, and the more I prayed it, the more I liked it. I especially liked praying it as I walked from Capuchin College to the National Shrine of the Immaculate Conception, as you can't get much more Marian than that. Reconnecting with Our Lady was great, and I loved meditating on the life of her Son on my daily walks.

After a few months of praying with it, my rosary broke. The cord snapped. So I sent the loose beads back to Alison. She fixed it and had it back to me a week later. That happened twice before she finally restrung the entire rosary with some unbreakable fishing line. While my rosary was "in the shop," I used a finger rosary that my mom used to keep in the ashtray of her car. To this day, that's the rosary I pray with whenever I have a drive longer than fifteen minutes.

I guess I shouldn't be surprised that I enjoy praying the Rosary, as both my parents had a deep devotion to Our Lady. They often used to end their dates with a visit to a Marian Shrine on Brookpark Road in Cleveland, which is where my dad proposed to my mom. But I was surprised that for about five years I had lost my Marian devotion, and I wanted to know why. It took an eight-day silent retreat in Nebraska to find my answer.

Remember that my mom died in 2001, a little more than a year before I was ordained a priest. Somewhere right around the time she died, I backed off from my relationship with Jesus' mother. Why? I couldn't tell you then. It just happened. But now that time has passed, I can tell you that human relationships can affect our relationship with God, and even his mother.

Somewhere deep within my heart I was afraid that, just as I lost my mom, I would somehow lose Mary, because she too was my mom, and my heart wasn't ready for any more pain. I realize now that such a fear was completely irrational, for we believe that Mary was assumed body and soul into heaven and lives forever. But the fear was still real, and I felt every bit of it. Moreover, I responded to it, maybe not with full intention or complete consent, but I did pull away from the Mother of God out of fear.

Fear is from the evil one. The devil wants us to live in the darkness of fear. Faith calls us into the light, to live in relationship with God and all his angels and saints, and in particular, his Mother Mary. Mary is also the model of the Church. She is the one who shows us how to receive Jesus and then how to share him with the world. Without her example, without her *fiat*, the incarnation would be an abstraction.

That Mary is both Virgin and Mother is a mystery. That God became a human being in Mary's womb in the person of Jesus Christ is just as much of a mystery. And that Jesus began an incarnational Church two thousand years ago that is truly the Bride of Christ while at the same time comprised of sinners like you and me, is equally mysterious. Ultimately, Catholicism is about God living his mystery in you and through you, just as he lived his mystery in and through Mary. Will you let it be?

Mary, Mother of Mercy, ora pro nobis.

Acknowledgments

MY MOM AND DAD created me sometime in the spring of 1975, and they had me recreated in the waters of Baptism on February 29, 1976. I'm forever grateful to them for that and for being my first and best teachers in the ways of faith. Without them this book wouldn't exist, because I wouldn't exist.

When we were growing up, most people thought my brother would be the priest. Adam was quiet, smart, hardworking, and respectful. He still is. He's a good husband and father too. Adam, I hope you enjoy this book, especially the parts about you.

I have to thank the Sisters of the Incarnate Word who educated me for nine very formative years of my life. I came to understand the beauty and the joy and the reality of the incarnation through all of you, especially my teachers. Thank you for seeing my hyperactivity as a gift from God and for being patient with me as a growing boy. I also want to thank you for making me write a lot as a kid. It has proven very helpful as an adult.

If you've already read this book, then you know that I wasn't much into the "school" part of high school in the early nineties. But Holy Name High School was very good to me, nonetheless. I had some great teachers who really loved me and a wonderful chaplain in Father Krizner who showed me the human face of Christ's priesthood, which made it possible for me to enter the seminary shortly after graduation.

I always tell people that Father Krizner got me into the seminary and Father Carlin kept me there. I'd like to thank Father Carlin and all the good people of Saint Charles Borromeo Parish in Parma, Ohio, for meeting me where I was as an eighteen-year-old seminarian and loving me into a priest. I'd also like to thank Father Lajak and all the faithful of Saint Wendelin Parish in Cleveland where my life of faith began. Special thanks to my godparents Jim and Mary Chura for their consistent witness, love, and support.

Many thanks to the Northcoast Spirit TEC community for immersing me in the Paschal Mystery, for teaching me contemplative prayer, and for making countless disciples in Northeast Ohio.

When I entered Borromeo Seminary in the fall of 1994, I wasn't certain that I was called to the priesthood, but I figured that the seminary was the place to find an answer. I never imagined that I'd return to Borromeo to teach philosophy or serve as the director of human formation, but the Lord is funny like that. And speaking of Borromeo, I must acknowledge the wonderful men who are in formation at our little college seminary in Cleveland. You guys are good, smart, faithful, holy, and very human young men, and I am a better priest for knowing you. If the Lord is calling you to the priesthood, please give him your *fiat* and know that I look forward to calling you my brother priests someday. And if he isn't, know that your time spent at Borromeo will make you a better man for his Kingdom. I also want to thank my brothers and sisters on the Borromeo Seminary faculty for being excellent at what you do in forming the next generation of Catholic priests.

Very warm thanks to Father Tom Johns for giving me the space to see where the Holy Spirit has been at work or where I need to let him work in my life. You are a gift.

To my Franciscan brothers of the Capuchin Province of Saint Augustine, thank you for your fraternity, hospitality, kindness, and for loving me as your brother in Christ.

To the School of Philosophy at the Catholic University of America, thanks for making me a better reader, a better writer, a better thinker, and for insisting that I make good distinctions.

To Bishop Robert Barron and everyone at Word on Fire, thanks for all you have done and continue to do to evangelize the culture and for allowing me to be a part of your most important movement.

Thanks to the ten friends who made the time to read this manuscript and who offered me some wonderful analysis, edits, commentary, and critique: Devon Lynch-Huggins-Szep, Jean Ann Montagna, Jen Nigito, Brad Mathisen, Danny O'Brien, Dr. Beth Rath, Father Patrick Schultz, Father Kevin Klonowski, transitional deacon Marty Dober, and Jon Hawkins.

I have some very good friends who have contributed to the writing of this book in one way or another. Thanks to my childhood friends for keeping me honest and letting me be a part of your families. Thanks to my First Friday priest support group for making me think outside of the ecclesial box of my generation. Thanks to my brothers at Casa Wojtyla for always keeping it real. Thanks to my young friends from {TOLLE LEGE} and all the good young people I've met through LifeTeen and Covecrest in particular. Thanks to my young-adult friends in the Diocese of Cleveland who make being a priest a great joy. Thanks to all my dedicated, hard-working, tireless, and faithful brother priests of the Diocese of Cleveland. And many thanks to Bishop Perez for being a good shepherd and for writing the foreword to this book.

In some ways this book is too conservative for liberals and too liberal for conservatives, which is a good sign that it's a Catholic book. Thank you, Pauline Books & Media, for your willingness to publish my first book. Special thanks to Sister Marianne Lorraine Trouve, FSP; Sister Christina M. Wegendt, FSP; and Vanessa Reese for your professionalism, faithfulness, and all the hard work you put into this project. Thanks to Mary Kate Glowe for the photo on the back cover and for your unfailing friendship.

To everyone who endorsed this book, thank you for reading the manuscript and for your kind words about it.

I want to extend a most heartfelt thanks to all my "Dear Young Friends" from my first parish youth group at Saint Mary's in Hudson, Ohio. I never had little siblings until I met you. I love you very much and I thought of you often as I wrote this book. And thanks to Father Kordas and all the faithful of Saint Mary's Parish. You taught me how to be a priest and I am forever indebted to you.

I'd also like to thank all the good people who make up the Diocese of Cleveland. You helped form me as a priest and you continue to make and support all kinds of disciples for the Kingdom. Cleveland rocks. You rock. I love you.

To the Triune God, thanks for creating the world and everything in it and for redeeming it after the Fall. And Mary, Our Lady, thank you for being the most beautiful woman ever and for being my friend.

Appendix 1

The Funeral Homily for Edward M. Ference

Including the homily I preached at my dad's funeral Mass as an appendix to this book was not my idea. It came from a few friends who read my manuscript and who also attended my dad's funeral Mass. They thought that making his funeral homily available to you, my reader, would greatly benefit you in your journey of faith. My friends thought that the homily did a good job showing, not just telling, what Catholicism looks like when lived well, which has been one of my primary reasons for writing this book. My dad showed me the "why" of Catholicism in his living, but also in his dying. Perhaps this homily, which I preached at my Dad's funeral on May 31, 2016 at 11:00 am at Saint Charles Borromeo Parish—Parma, Ohio, Diocese of Cleveland—will show that to you too.

THE REASON WE ARE here today, my brothers and sisters, is not simply because my dad died. You may think that's why you are here, but there's more to it. Trust me. We are all here because Jesus Christ—who is true God and true Man—suffered, died, and rose from the dead. Yet you may say, "Yeah, yeah. I know that your dad was super Catholic and that you are a priest and all, but I'm actually here because your dad died, regardless of his faith in Christ. He was a good guy and I want to pay my respects." But I need to say, unequivocally, that my dad's life wouldn't make any sense apart from the life, death, and resurrection of Jesus.

Here's the background: Before there was anything—plants, animals, humans, planets, atoms, molecules, whatever—there was God: Father, Son, and Spirit—a communion of Persons. God created the world and everything in it, and the best of his creation was the human race—male and female he created them. We humans were created in the image and likeness of God, which means that we are like God in a way nothing else in creation is. We have intellect (we can know), we have will (we can choose), and we have bodies, and our bodies matter, as we'll see in a bit.

We know the story. Our first parents, rather than choosing to be in relationship, friendship, harmony with God, decided to break that friendship and see God as their competitor, no longer as their friend and Creator. We call that sin. So the rest of the Old Testament is an account of God trying to bring his people back into communion with him. In the fullness of time God the Father sent his Son to be born of a virgin named Mary. Now at this point you may say, "Yes, Father, we know. You're talking about Christmas." And you are right. But here's where I think we often get way too comfortable.

Unlike our Jewish brothers and sisters and our Muslim brothers and sisters who also believe in one God, Christians actually believe that God became a human being. Not an angel, but a human being. That means that God took on a human body like yours, yet remained God. How humbling. If you haven't thought about how wild a teaching the incarnation is, think about it. God, who is pure spirit, all-good, all-knowing, all-powerful, all-loving, decided to become like one of us. He became incarnate. He took on flesh. And why did he do that? Because that original sin of our first parents separated us from God and brought about death. In Jesus, God takes on human flesh to bring us life, to bring us salvation, to bring us God! Here's how Saint Athanasius put it, "God became man so that man could become God."

It gets better. It's not only that God became a human being in the person of Jesus, but that he also went through everything that we human beings go through. He was born of a woman, he was part of a family, he had a job as a carpenter, he had good friends, and he enjoyed being with people, especially around a table. But he also knew the tougher aspects of life. He knew what it was like to be tempted, mocked, denied, betrayed, beaten, scourged, left alone. He knew what it was like to suffer and to die. And remember, this is God we are talking about, who became one of us in all things but sin. In the person of Jesus Christ, God comes to us to experience everything we experience including death itself, which is why in most Catholic churches you will find a big old crucifix on the back wall of the church. It's not because we are sick, demented, or masochistic, but to remind us that Jesus is Emmanuel—God with us—not only in the cradle of Bethlehem, but on the cross of Calvary as well.

So Jesus died, just like my dad died early Thursday morning. And if you have loved ones who have died, know that Jesus died just as they did. God with us. He keeps himself from nothing. He enters all things human, even and especially death itself. But three days later Jesus rose from the dead, never to die again. And you may say, "Yeah, I know the story, that's Easter." But let's really ponder the resurrection for a moment. When someone dies, that's it. That's the end. You can remember them and tell nice stories, but until the resurrection of Jesus, there was no reason to believe that you'd actually ever see that person again. Jesus rose from the dead, not as an angel or a pure spirit, but with his body—his glorified body. So it was like your body and mine, but different. In a sense, the resurrected body is MORE REAL than the bodies we have now. And Jesus told his disciples, with his own body, that if they follow him in death, then they will also follow him to eternal life. That's the story. That's why we're here today. My dad believed in the resurrection of the dead. He believed that Jesus conquered death and opened the gates to eternal life.

In the first reading today we heard from the First Book of Samuel. God calls Samuel but he's confused. He thinks it's Eli calling him. But eventually he figures it out and tells God, "Speak, LORD, your servant is listening" (see 1 Sam 3:10). And Samuel became an "accredited prophet" of the Lord. In Baptism, way back in 1924, Edward Michael Ference died with Christ and rose with him to new life in the waters of Baptism at Saint Wendelin Church. His body got wet, and he received his call to holiness, to follow Jesus—to live in Jesus and to allow Jesus to live in him. My dad's conversion process didn't all happen at once, but it did happen, and that was the day that it started.

In the Second Reading we heard from Saint Paul. He starts out, "Consider your own calling, brothers and sisters" (1 Cor 1:26). Again, we hear "the call." Often as Catholics, when we talk about "the call" or "vocations," we think of priests and religious, but that's only half the story. Every Christian is called to be another Christ. Remember what Saint Athanasius used to say: "God became man so that man could become God." And God chose my dad, who by human standards was not wise, powerful, or of noble birth. (He was, after all, the son of Slovak peasants.) What did God want from my dad? To live in him. To incarnate himself in him. To present Jesus to the world through the person of Eddie Ference.

How does that work? Here's how. Just as God didn't come to save us as an angel, but with a body, so too God makes some stuff of this world holy in order to make us more like him. He brings us into his family through water, consecrates us and heals us through oil, by the power of the Holy Spirit he turns bread and wine into his Body and Blood, takes a body like mine and calls me to be a priest, takes bodies like my mom's and dad's and says this is what my relationship with my people looks like in holy matrimony. It's the sacramental life. God enters into our lives in very tangible ways. He is not distant. He is close. He is one of us. He is God with us, Emmanuel.

Some of you don't know this, but many do—my dad was a daily Mass-goer up until about the last month of his life, when he could no longer get out of bed. Every morning he would enter into the Paschal Mystery of Jesus, by calling to mind his sins, asking God for mercy, then listening to his word, and eating his Body and drinking his Blood. (It's also worth noting that he reflected daily on the Joyful, Sorrowful, Glorious, and Luminous Mysteries of Christ's life with his Rosary.) What did all this do for my dad? It made him another Christ. In our Gospel we heard Jesus telling his disciples to be salt and light. Why? Because our fallen world is flat, flavorless, dark, and sad. Who is the light of the world? Jesus. How does he make his presence known in the world today? Through his community of disciples, which we call the Church. My dad was part of that Church.

At the end of today's Gospel we heard this, "Your light must shine before others, that they may see your good deeds and glorify your heavenly Father" (Mt 5:16).

One of the dismissals at the end of Mass goes like this: "Go in peace, glorifying the Lord by your life." You see what's happening? The whole point of God becoming one of us in the person of Jesus Christ is that we might become like him, so that when people see me, they actually see Jesus. God became a human being so that human beings might become God.

There are a lot of ways that my dad glorified God by his life, from his marriage, to his fatherhood, his military service, and I could go on and on. But I want to talk about two ways in particular that he glorified God by his life, because I think they are very important.

First, my dad was a construction worker—Local 17—an elevator mechanic. You know what happens on constructions sites? Other than constructing, two things are the most common—bad language and degrading talk about women. In my forty years of life I only heard my dad swear once (in a joke, and it wasn't even that bad) and I never heard him talk degradingly about women. He even canceled his subscription to a sports magazine so that Adam and I wouldn't be malformed by the swimsuit issue. So when my dad walked onto the construction site after going to daily Mass, not cussing or talking badly about women, who was walking on that construction site? Yep. Jesus. The Second Vatican Council said that it was the job of the laity to bring Jesus to parts of the world that only they could, to be salt and light—to be Jesus. My dad did that on the construction site. He brought Jesus there. Like Samuel he was an accredited prophet.

Second, at the heart of Christian life is the *emptying of self*. God so loved the world that he gave us his only Son, and Jesus so loved us that he gave his life away for us. There's a nice Greek word for self-emptying, self-giving, self-donating love—*kenosis*. After my mom died, my dad lived for twelve years in his house on Thornton Drive as a legally blind man. My mom had the foresight to adapt the house to his poor vision, and he made a go of it, walking to Mass every day here at Saint Charles and living a good independent life. But when his heart took a turn a couple of years back, and when we realized that he needed twenty-four-hour care, Adam and I moved him to Mount Alverna Village. It's right next to Holy Family Home, where my mom spent the last year of her life. (The Dominicans took care of my mom and the Franciscans took care of my dad. Pretty cool.) It was not an easy transition. He had to let go of his home, independence, and even his money. Like Jesus, he emptied himself. But if you knew my dad, you would know that he did so joyfully. Sure, some days were tough, but he clung to his faith and lived to be salt and light to anyone he would meet, especially those who bathed him, changed him, fed him, and gave him his meds at Mount Alverna. He showed Jesus to others in himself.

These last few weeks were pretty tough at Mount Alverna. Adam and I talked about how hard it was to see the strongest man in our life become the weakest. But again, think of Jesus. He was a strong carpenter, but he suffered terribly and died a violent death as his mother looked on. When someone is suffering or dying, or both, our gut reaction may be to ignore it, run from it, or do something to stop it. But because God became one of us in Jesus Christ, our suffering now has meaning. There's a deep mystery to suffering. It's not something you solve like a math problem or figure out like a puzzle. It's a mystery, and when you enter into it with faith, it figures you out, it solves you. That mystery is Jesus Christ. As I sat with my dad as he lay on his deathbed, which was his cross, I sat with sadness, but also with real hope. I had hope because a few days before my dad died he told me and Father Mark Riley that "I am going to see Jesus, my salvation, and my wife, Joannie Bologna!" (Note that he got the order right.) He knew who he was and he knew whose he was.

One last thought and then we'll continue our Mass. In 2009 my dad joined a plane full of World War II veterans on an honor flight to Washington, D.C., to visit the World War II Memorial on the National Mall. He and a bunch of the Greatest Generation landed at BWI, wearing the same light blue T-shirts, identifying them as World War II veterans. The folks at the airport announced that the veterans had just arrived. The way my dad told the story, all through the airport, from the time the guys walked off the jetway until they got into their limo bus, people stood, clapped, saluted, and cheered. My dad would get teary-eyed every time he told that story. I like that image, and I think it's a good way to close this homily. My prayer for my dad is that he receives that same sort of greeting from the angels and saints in eternity, that Jesus recognizes himself in my dad and burns away anything in my dad that has not yet been purged from him by Jesus' fiery love, and that Jesus welcomes him into the Promised Land.

My dad wasn't perfect, but he was a disciple. May the same be said of you and of me when it's our time for judgment.

Appendix 2

Questions for Discussion and Personal Reflection

God Is for Us, God Is with Us

Incarnation

1. Many people believe that God is in competition with their freedom, their happiness, their joy, and their autonomy. Why is such an understanding of God problematic?

2. Why do you think it's typically easier for people to think of God being with us and for us in the cradle of Bethlehem (good times) than on the cross of Calvary (bad times)?

3. Have you ever experienced God being with you and for you?

The Empty Tomb
Resurrection

1. Have you ever lost to death someone you loved? Who was it? What did you go through? How has that loss affected you?

2. How is resuscitation different from resurrection? Why does it matter?

3. Why did Jesus have to experience death in order to save us from death?

4. Hoping that one day you will join the angels and saints in heaven, what do you most look forward to about your own glorified body?

Matter Matters
Sacramentality

1. The Catholic worldview holds that creation is good, matter is good, and bodies are good. Do you agree with that view?

2. How are the incarnation and the Sacraments related?

3. Why does God choose to make himself sacramentally present through things like water, bread, wine, oil, and human bodies? Why does it matter?

Everybody Counts and Everyone Matters
The Human Person

1. The celebrities of Catholic Christianity look a lot different than the celebrities of pop culture. Why?

2. What is the difference between valuing a human life by what it is as opposed to what it is able to do?

3. The philosopher John Paul Sartre is famous for saying, "Hell is other people." For the Christian, other people are Jesus Christ. Discuss.

Show and Tell
Exemplarity

1. Human beings learn better by being shown rather than by being told what to do. Can you offer an example of this principle working in your own life through a parent, teacher, coach, mentor, or friend?

2. Jesus shows us—he doesn't just tell us—what God is like, and what humanity looks like when it is united with God. Why is this unique to a Christian understanding of God?

3. Saints are people who present Jesus Christ to the world in their persons. Who are your favorite saints? What is keeping you from being a saint?

Take Up and Read
The Beautiful and Intelligent Life

1. The Catholic Church takes beauty very seriously, which is often on display in its architecture, stained glass, sacred vessels, ornate vestments, and liturgical music. Where have you experienced the beauty of Catholicism?

2. If the Catholic Church is a Church for the poor, what is the justification for the Church possessing so much priceless art

and owning so many opulent churches while so many people around the world live in poverty?

3. Christian faith, as seen in the life of Saint Augustine, has the ability to broaden one's reason and is not in competition with it. Discuss.

A Vivid World
The Both/And Principle

1. What is your favorite iteration of the both/and principle on display in Catholicism?

2. What problems might the both/and principle pose to America's two-party political system?

3. A major critique of religion is that it is somehow anti-science. Is this a valid criticism of Catholic Christianity? What is the relationship between faith and reason according to Catholicism?

Loving the Bomb
An Answer to Suffering

1. If you are old enough to be reading this book, chances are that you have suffered. Discuss your experience of suffering. Were you able to find any meaning in it?

2. Many people deny God's existence due to the problem of suffering, especially of innocent/good people. What do you think of Christianity's response to suffering, as presented in the Paschal Mystery?

3. What does it mean to *love the bomb* and why is *loving the bomb* counterintuitive?

Appendix 3
Further Reading

If you enjoyed this book and are looking to read some of the books that have influenced my life, my faith, and my Catholic imagination, here are twelve that I think you might enjoy.

Aristotle. *Nicomachean Ethics*. 2nd ed. Translated by Terence Irwin. Indianapolis: Hackett Publishing Company, Inc., 1999.

Augustine. *Confessions*. Translated by John K. Ryan. New York: Image Books, 1960.

Barron, Robert. *The Strangest Way: Walking the Christian Path*. New York: Orbis Books, 2002.

Day, Dorothy. *The Long Loneliness: The Autobiography of Dorothy Day*. San Francisco: Harper San Francisco, 1952.

Elie, Paul. *The Life You Save May Be Your Own: An American Pilgrimage*. New York: Farrar, Straus and Giroux, 2003.

Lewis, C. S. *Mere Christianity*. San Francisco: Harper San Francisco, 1952.

O'Connor, Flannery. *The Habit of Being: Letters of Flannery O'Connor*. Selected and edited by Sally Fitzgerald. New York: Farrar, Straus and Giroux, 1979.

Ratzinger, Joseph. *Introduction to Christianity*. 2nd ed. Translated by J. R. Foster. San Francisco: Ignatius Press, 2004.

Springsteen, Bruce. *Born to Run*. New York: Simon and Schuster, 2016.

Toole, John Kennedy. *A Confederacy of Dunces*. New York: Grove Press, 1980.

Weil, Simone. *Waiting for God*. New York: Harper Collins, 1973.

Wilken, Robert Louis. *The Spirit of Early Christian Thought: Seeking the Face of God*. New Haven: Yale University Press, 2003.

Notes

Chapter 1

1. For additional reflection on the Trinity, start with articles 238–260 of the *Catechism of the Catholic Church*. There are many good books on the Trinity, but I find that sitting with the Church's most basic teachings on a topic is often most efficacious.

2. Remember that God creates through his Word. What God says happens. God said, "Let there be light" and there was light. The Second Person of the Trinity is also known as God's Word. The Incarnate Word, then, means that the Second Person of the Trinity became a human being in the person of Jesus Christ.

Chapter 2

1. Pius XII, *Mediator Dei*, 39 (1947) 548.

Chapter 4

1. This community was founded by Nathaniel Hawthorne's daughter, Rose Hawthorne, on the lower east side of Manhattan. It was established to take care of the poor who were dying of cancer.

2. Robert Barron, *The Strangest Way: Walking the Christian Path* (New York: Orbis Books, 2002), 159.

Chapter 5

1. Benedict XVI, *Deus Caritas Est* (Boston: Pauline Books & Media, 2006), 1.

2. The German word translated as *tug* is *zug,* which is derived from the verb *ziehen*, which means to draw, drag, or pull. It is also worth noting that *zug* is one translation for the English word *train*, which draws, drags, tugs, and pulls a line of cars. It is in this spirit that Scheler explains how the model person *tugs* or *draws* the agent toward him.

3. Augustine, *Confessions*, trans. John K. Ryan (New York: Image Books, 1960), 9.vii.

4. Ibid., 6.xv.

5. Ibid., 8.vii.

Chapter 6

1. Robert Louis Wilken, *The Spirit of Early Christian Thought: Seeing the Face of God* (New Haven: Yale University Press, 2003), 241.

2. Ibid., 240.

3. Ibid., 241.

Chapter 8

1. Joel Lovell "The Late, Great Stephen Colbert," *Gentleman's Quarterly* (August 17, 2015) http://www.gq.com/story/stephen-colbert-gq-cover-story.

2. Ibid.

3. Ibid.

4. Ibid.

BOOKS & MEDIA

The Daughters of St. Paul operate book and media centers at the following addresses. Visit, call, or write the one nearest you today, or find us at www.paulinestore.org.

CALIFORNIA
3908 Sepulveda Blvd, Culver City, CA 90230 — 310-397-8676
3250 Middlefield Road, Menlo Park, CA 94025 — 650-562-7060

FLORIDA
145 S.W. 107th Avenue, Miami, FL 33174 — 305-559-6715

HAWAII
1143 Bishop Street, Honolulu, HI 96813 — 808-521-2731

ILLINOIS
172 North Michigan Avenue, Chicago, IL 60601 — 312-346-4228

LOUISIANA
4403 Veterans Memorial Blvd, Metairie, LA 70006 — 504-887-7631

MASSACHUSETTS
885 Providence Hwy, Dedham, MA 02026 — 781-326-5385

MISSOURI
9804 Watson Road, St. Louis, MO 63126 — 314-965-3512

NEW YORK
115 E. 29th Street, New York City, NY 10016 — 212-754-1110

SOUTH CAROLINA
243 King Street, Charleston, SC 29401 — 843-577-0175

TEXAS
No book center; for parish exhibits or outreach evangelization, contact: 210-569-0500, or SanAntonio@paulinemedia.com, or P.O. Box 761416, San Antonio, TX 78245

VIRGINIA
1025 King Street, Alexandria, VA 22314 — 703-549-3806

CANADA
3022 Dufferin Street, Toronto, ON M6B 3T5 — 416-781-9131

¡También somos su fuente para libros,
videos y música en español!